LET 'EM HOWL

"Pat's peerless mastery of political organization and deep commitment to progressive politics has made her one of Canadian politics' secret weapons. And the cut-the-crap directness that has deflated more than one puffed-up politician or self-serving staffer is on full display in this book. She tells her story—and its universal lessons for anyone wanting to make a real contribution in the world of politics—in typical Pat Sorbara style: with a steely eye, a sharp tongue, a big heart and, most of all, an uncompromising honesty."

– Peter Donolo, Vice-Chair Hill+Knowlton Canada, and former Director of Communications for Prime Minister Jean Chrétien

LET 'EM HOWL

Lessons from a Life in Backroom Politics

PAT SORBARA

Enjoy + always let them howl!
Pat S.
June 2023

NIGHTWOOD EDITIONS

2019

Nightwood Editions
P.O. Box 1779
Gibsons, BC VON IVO
Canada
www.nightwoodeditions.com

COVER DESIGN: Matthew Dupuis & Carleton Wilson
TYPESETTING: Carleton Wilson
COVER PHOTO: Jenna Muirhead

Canada

Nightwood Editions acknowledges the support of the Canada Council for the Arts, which last year invested $153 million to bring the arts to Canadians throughout the country.

Nous remercions le Conseil des arts du Canada de son soutien. L'an dernier, le Conseil a investi 153 millions de dollars pour mettre de l'art dans la vie des Canadiennes et des Canadiens de tout le pays.

We also gratefully acknowledge financial support from the Government of Canada and from the Province of British Columbia through the BC Arts Council and the Book Publishing Tax Credit.

This book has been produced on 100% post-consumer recycled, ancient-forest-free paper, processed chlorine-free and printed with vegetable-based dyes.

Printed and bound in Canada.

LIBRARY AND ARCHIVES CANADA CATALOGUING IN PUBLICATION

Title: Let 'em howl : lessons from a life in backroom politics / Patricia Sorbara.
Names: Sorbara, Patricia, 1956- author.
Identifiers: Canadiana (print) 20190127368 | Canadiana (ebook) 20190127384 | ISBN 9780889713581 (softcover) | ISBN 9780889711488 (ebook)
Subjects: LCSH: Sorbara, Patricia, 1956- | LCSH: Political consultants—Ontario—Biography. | LCSH: Women political consultants—Ontario—Biography. | LCSH: Ontario—Officials and employees—Biography.
Classification: LCC FC3079.1.S67 A3 2019 | DDC 971.3/05092—dc23

*   *   *

In acknowledgement of every person, regardless of party, who signed up to be a political staffer somewhere along the way. Never doubt that your time in the backrooms of politics, campaigns and government made a difference. You are unsung heroes, in every way possible.

Contents

Introduction

I have been a person of politics for more than forty years. It's been my passion. I've put in hundreds of hours as a volunteer and I've worked as a staff person at many levels, both provincially and federally—moving up the ranks from constituency assistant to the campaign director and chief executive officer of the Ontario Liberal Party. Even when I stepped away from it completely, to pursue a different career path, it pulled me back. Over and over. It has always been there—in my head, in my heart, in my subconscious. And while I think it's partly because I'm very good at it, I know it's mostly because I believed, from a very early age, that government matters—and by extension, politics matters, too. Ultimately it meant that I was destined to be a political lifer.

I was always aware of the phrase "women in politics" and to be honest, it was odd to me. In the earliest years I was obviously cognizant of how few women were elected officials but in the part of the political world in which I was operating, the majority of the people who did the work—in the background and in campaigns—were women. When I started my career in the late 1970s and early 1980s, women in general were still being discouraged from putting their careers ahead of all else. But in politics, women were beginning to wield significant influence behind the scenes. All you had to do was ask the male politicians whom they counted on the most. There was almost always a woman running the show in the backroom, and the smartest politicians didn't make a move without her okay.

Beyond that, the campaign offices were filled with women who did the manual work and ran the day-to-day. They executed key decisions, managed volunteers, trained canvassers and led the outreach to voters. But they also made meals and swept floors. They taught me how to recognize priorities and manage crises while, at the same time, it was made clear to me that no job was too small. They taught me it was always about getting the job done, whatever that required and however long that took. I learned an incredible amount at the feet of those women, and I loved every minute of it.

But after a while it became apparent to me that, while female role models were never lacking in the backroom, what was lacking was the number of women who sat at the table—and who had a voice—where the decisions were being made. The table didn't matter—whether they were tables in campaign offices, the caucus room or the cabinet table, there weren't enough of us. And I wanted to help change that.

Much has been written in recent years about cracking the glass ceiling, which in politics almost always refers to elected women. It has been thrilling to watch the change around women running for office. I started recruiting female candidates in the days when the comments would run along the lines of, "*The voters of this riding will never elect a woman*," or "*There are no qualified women in this riding.*" That's why it was so meaningful to me to have had a significant role in electing the first woman leader of a mainstream political party in Ontario and years later, to hold the second-most senior role on the team that won the fight to elect the first woman premier of Ontario.

Little did I know that just months after electing that woman, I'd find myself in a position I never imagined I'd face. In December 2014, my cover as a backroom operative far from the public eye was blown completely when it was announced I was being investigated in relation to ostensibly bribing a potential candidate to step down in a nomination race in Sudbury, Ontario. Suddenly I was catapulted to the front pages of the newspapers and lead-off questions in question period.

* * *

The first day of my trial—September 7, 2017—held in a heritage courthouse in Sudbury, was my sixty-first birthday. As I walked into the courtroom for the first time, one of my lawyers, Erin Dann, turned to me and said, "There's something I should have mentioned sooner."

I'd be required to enter a plea. Erin quickly explained that both counts against me would be read out by the clerk, and I would need to respond, "Not guilty." I was to sound confident and calm, and to look directly at the judge when I said those two words.

I was, in fact, confident. But while I felt calm as I entered the courtroom, I had not prepared myself for that moment (I was prepared for a hundred other moments, but not that one!). As I heard the first count being read, a surge of emotion surfaced, but I had to push through and focus on the task at hand. Other than when Premier Kathleen Wynne took the stand, and when the judge delivered his final verdict forty-seven days from the start of the trial, this was the most intense moment of the experience for me. My breathing became a bit erratic and tears threatened. It became much bigger than having to answer what seemed like a simple question: "How do you plead?"

It was in that moment that I alone had to answer. Reality crashed down, and I had no choice but to discard my disbelief at actually standing before a judge.

I spared a thought for my long-time therapist, the late Dr. Ralph Bierman, who taught me how to manage my anxiety. I reached deep and slowed my breathing. It felt a little like what people describe as your life flashing before your eyes in the moment of a sudden death. In this case, it was my political life flashing before my eyes. I had survived every major challenge I'd encountered, because I had learned to believe in myself, and to trust my gut and what I knew to be true.

I thought of all the people who believed in me. In the room was my good friend Kathy Robinson and my strong legal team. Family and friends who were angry and frustrated on my behalf had gone out of their way to be sure I knew how much faith they had in me, and in my integrity. And there was my Liberal family, most of whom had supported me from the first moment the so-called "Sudbury scandal" took root.

It did not take long to reach the place I needed to go. I had been there before. I refused to allow the doubt of others, the nastiness, the mean-spirited intent to do damage, to overtake what I knew in my gut. I was innocent, and I would be proven innocent.

In a clear, confident voice—but with my heart pounding in my chest—I responded "Not guilty" to both counts. Erin later said the tone was perfect, genuine. People often seem shocked when someone sounds genuine. The simple reality is that it's easy to be that authentic when you believe what you are saying, when you're telling the truth. The trick is to figure out where that conviction lives. Mine came from a place inside of me that existed only because of years and years of fighting the battles as they came along—and learning the lessons that came with those battles—and never giving into those who wanted me or my cause to fail. It's the place that my hero Nellie McClung was referring to when she said, "Never retract, never explain, never apologize—get the thing done and let them howl!" I was a warrior and I would win this battle no matter who was howling, and regardless of the fact that this was the most public fight of my career.

The Sudbury saga was major for me of course, but truth be told, had I returned to work as if it had not happened, it probably would have faded into another chapter in my compendium of career lessons. What happened after the charges were dismissed, though—when I tried to return to my place in the Ontario Liberal Party—was a whole different story. That experience motivated me to document what it's like for a person who has dedicated much of their life to partisan politics. After all, what else was I going to do when I found myself sitting on the sidelines as my party self-destructed in the 2018 campaign in Ontario, when Kathleen Wynne joined the ranks of strong women who failed to be re-elected?

My intention in writing this book is not to name names (though that will happen in the course of my storytelling) but to draw from my experience to share the best lessons I learned in the backroom—the ones that sustained me in both the brightest and darkest hours of my career. It's my hope that this book will become required reading of sorts for anyone considering a career in politics or as political staff in government, so they come to understand the highs and lows that await them.

But the lessons aren't just for the politically inclined. What I've learned crosses industries and positions and is especially relevant for any woman who envisions herself at the helm of something big—even if she intends to direct the show from behind the curtain. In fact, maybe this book should actually be called *How to Let 'Em Howl*. Because if I can teach the next generation of political staffers, especially women, anything, it should be that.

CHAPTER 1

Bloom Where You're Planted

"The formula for success is simple: do your best and someone
might like it."
– Marva Collins

There are many routes into politics. Some people come for a single purpose, like supporting someone they believe in, or pursuing a specific issue they feel strongly about. Some look to bring about a change in government, or decide to run for election. For some it starts as an internship or a job. But a much smaller group have been "called" to serve a partisan cause. They love the political world and are at home in it. I fall into the latter category.

Regardless of how you get involved, or how long you stay, there is no world like it. It is certainly not for everyone. Just like you can't be an emergency room doctor if you faint at the sight of blood, you won't survive politics if you cannot deal with the behind-the-scenes reality of how partisan politics works. Chaos is the norm, but it is a manageable chaos if the hierarchy, structure and discipline are in place to handle things as they come at you. It's critical that people are in place to triage the "incoming" and determine priorities.

It takes a strong operation, a team of people who understand the overall imperative of the organization, and clear, concise direction from the Centre. (In government, "the Centre" is either the Premier's Office or Prime Minister's Office, or if you're in opposition, the Leader's Office. Within political parties, it means the leadership group at the central party or the central campaign.)

But the bottom line is if you can find a way to endure the ups and downs of winning versus losing (because there are almost certainly more downs than ups), it is an exciting, enriching and extraordinarily fascinating world, conducted mostly in backrooms. But that endurance will require you to give your all, no matter how big or small the task. It's not about the glory, it's about your contribution.

Lesson: You may not like the assignment, or you may have envisioned a different role for yourself, but by giving the task your best, you will always win, regardless of the outcome.

I became a Liberal early in life. In 1968, I was in grade six at Sacred Heart School in Guelph, Ontario. The school was in the heart of "the Ward"—ward one, and the part of town where many Italians first came to live when they immigrated to Canada. The immigrant wave from Italy settled in many towns across southern Ontario, including Guelph. My grandfather and grandmother came in 1912 and 1913, respectively. They met, married, and their eight children were raised in this neighbourhood. I never knew my grandfather, Sam Sorbara, as he died unexpectedly and in grim circumstances when his youngest child was only a few months old.

My grandmother persisted, in a very challenging situation. She is the first female role model I remember, and in today's terms she would have been rightly bestowed the title "badass." I'm not sure she'd approve of the independent woman I became—divorced, no children, career-oriented, family more distant than she would have ever allowed. Regardless, I saw in her a strong woman in control of her world. She raised her fatherless kids in the best way she could, with no money and at a time the world was struggling through a global war.

Concetta Sorbara, my nonna (or Nonie, as my family called her), was a strong, disciplined matriarch who taught her children and grandchildren that family came first. In those days, priests, parents and teachers held great sway and kids were never right. You did what you were told, and you certainly did not talk back to authority. And women were meant to obey their husbands.

She went to mass daily and her faith (and all the other grand-mothers dressed in black) got her through. When I would show up on a weekday morning and sit with her in church, she would proudly boast to her friends that I would become a nun. When I got a bit older, I told her boldly my choice was to be a priest and not a nun, as priests get to make all the decisions. She let me know such a sugges-tion was not remotely proper... or funny.

1968. Ring a bell? It was the year Pierre Trudeau first ran in a federal election, having succeeded Lester B. Pearson as leader of the Liberal Party of Canada. By this point, I was twelve and I'd been fol-lowing politics and current events for a while. I regularly watched the news with my dad, as he was adamant that I pay attention to what was happening in the world. (This was a man who, despite leaving school at an early age, read three newspapers a day.) I remember he and I had even watched the many rounds of the Liberal leadership convention on television over a weekend in April 1968. Whether it was inherited or through youthful exposure, or both, the political bug took root in me early.

That June my teacher, Don Drone, announced we would be hav-ing a mock election and I was thrilled when chosen as one of three students who would be candidates. But I was supremely annoyed when it was announced I would be representing the NDP. After los-ing an argument with Mr. Drone (if you can call it an argument—I was insistent I just *had* to be the Liberal), I went home and com-plained loudly to my dad. How could I be the NDP candidate when I was a Liberal, just like him?

My dad believed in doing the best you could with the hand you were dealt. He inherited that from his mother. My parents urged me and my four sisters to excel at whatever we did. Actually, we were given little choice. As far as my parents were concerned, hard work and discipline could tackle any issue. School mattered and if you were in trouble at school, you were in twice the trouble at home. When a report card in elementary school noted my handwriting needed work, I argued the teacher picked on my handwriting because they had little else negative to mention. It was an arrogant comment and it got the slap-down it deserved. For weeks after that report card, I was made to sit in front of the television balancing a large blackboard on the arms of my chair, writing out my alphabet. To this day people still comment that my handwriting is lovely.

Dad also believed in the absolute authority of the teacher. He reminded me that my NDP candidacy was a school assignment and like any other assignment I was given, I was to follow instructions and complete it to the best of my ability. In the end, the assignment turned into an excellent adventure. More than that, it deeply impacted my outlook as a young girl venturing forth in the real world of male-dominated politics. I was terrified and excited by the opportunity.

In the spirit of encouraging me to do my best, my dad made sure I understood the assignment beyond books and reading the news. Every few days throughout the campaign, he took me to the NDP campaign office. At that time, NDP campaigns were almost always run out of the local union office. Dad was a well-known and respected member of the plumbers and steamfitters' union, and union organizers readily embraced his request that they help me prepare for the school campaign. It was a world of important men, but they patiently explained their views to me, along with why they believed the Liberal and Conservative policies weren't working. I had to work hard to not be intimidated and to ask my questions with confidence. I felt accepted and looked forward to every visit.

Then something magical happened. NDP leader Tommy Douglas was coming to the area and the union leaders asked me to present flowers to Tommy's wife, Irma. I vividly remember the thrill of that moment. There was my new sage green and gold brocade, sleeveless dress, which in and of itself was unusual. As the third of five girls, almost all of my dresses were hand-me-downs. In semi-darkness, I stepped carefully over wires and cables backstage at the rally and made my way to face the large audience. There was the joy of presenting the flowers to Mrs. Douglas, then to proudly shake the hand of Tommy Douglas and hear him speak about Canada, aware of the impact he'd already had on our country. It was formational and foundational in its impact; to me as a young girl, it represented aspiration, and all that was right about politics.

Back at school, I ran a substantive campaign, making a strong, compelling speech to my classmates. However, it was impossible to overtake Trudeaumania and the strong Liberal support found in the local Italian community. The moment my loss to the Liberal candidate was announced, I reached over and snatched the button from my classmate's lapel, placing it on my own jacket and stating, "Now I can be a Liberal and I always will be."Truer words were never spoken.

I'm grateful to Mr. Drone for forcing me to look at politics from outside of my comfort zone. He has always believed in me and in that year, due to his encouragement, I gained a lot of confidence in myself.

It may have been fifty years ago but that exposure to real-world politics was such a moment for me. Although I did not fully realize it at the time, essentially my political career began in those first backrooms, hanging out with the tough guys in the union office and being rewarded for my earnest attempt at being the best NDP candidate I could be. I was given the opportunity to meet a Canadian political icon. I felt comfortable, I loved the intrigue and the nature of the political debate. I enjoyed hearing my dad banter with the NDP about their policies. I never looked back.

Of course, I had no idea of the barriers that existed for women generally, or in politics. I don't remember meeting a woman working in that campaign, other than the ones who got the coffee for Dad when we arrived at the union office. I know now it would have been those same women doing all the real work behind the scenes.

Lesson: Earn your stripes. There is always a campaign, a local organization, a candidate to support. Don't try to start at the top. The view from the bottom is just as riveting and the chance to make your mark is limitless.

In grade eight, at age fourteen, I won an election for the first time. I ran for president of the student council at St. James Catholic School, which was a middle school at the time. (My main competitor was my best friend, Rosemary Danielli. I often remark it was through that grade eight competition that we found our paths—mine into politics and Rosemary's into a medical career that demanded the highest academic achievement.)

By high school I was called upon regularly to organize whatever task needed attention. I was over-invested in many clubs and projects while managing to keep up on my academics. My parents began to hear the word "leader" when teachers talked about me, and I started to understand the pressure of being counted on to get things done.

I went to a Catholic high school at a time we were fighting the provincial government for funding equal to that of the public school system. Standing with thousands of students on the front lawn of Queen's Park, demanding justice from the Bill Davis Conservative government of the day, was a formative moment on my political journey. It was the first time I'd felt the power of the many demanding action on an issue that mattered deeply to them. It was an important side of politics to experience.

After graduation, I attended the University of Guelph. I didn't know anyone but I knew politics. I joined the Politics Club and the Liberal Club. I added a second major in political studies (along with my major in psychology and a minor in history) because I wanted to learn as much about the theory of politics as I was learning about the political ground game. I met a lot of people from all parties, including my future husband, Jim Whitechurch.

Studies were important but as there was always some campaign calling my name, I found a way to do both. I stuffed envelopes, canvassed door-to-door and by phone, and helped to organize the student vote. Sometimes I got to sit in on meetings to talk about the state of a campaign. I readily accepted any responsibility the campaign office workers were prepared to give me, whether it was making a chart or organizing a group of people. For several years I held the position of president of the local Liberal riding association in Wellington South (in those days it was a combined federal and provincial entity). I was earning my stripes.

Lesson: Look for role models who believe in you and are willing to let you learn.

There is a saying I like and use often: "You cannot be what you cannot see." It usually references a "first" for a woman—as in the first woman astronaut, first woman scientist to work at NASA, first woman director to win an Oscar, a woman candidate, a woman leading a major political party, a woman cabinet minister, a woman premier, a woman prime minister... More generally, it speaks to the breakthrough moment experienced by any woman making her way in a world dominated by men.

My formative years as an organizer were in Guelph. The Liberal organization there was run by strong, smart and incredibly passionate women, including Anne Dmetriuc, Fran Hunter, Irene Maschio, Linda Fordyce and Mary Rammage. Anne was our leader. She came from the "take no prisoners" school of politics. It was rare that anyone said no to her. She had a long memory and a deep belief in loyalty (like most of the Italians I grew up with), and it ran in both directions. Anne taught me much of what I know about campaigns but more importantly, she gave me the confidence to tackle the work of an organizer at a young age. She let me have as much responsibility as I was willing to take on—and I was willing to take on a lot.

In my first few campaigns, I quickly learned that my forte was ensuring the ground game was operational, and as efficient and effective as possible. This meant that I was tasked with directing the resources allocated to finding votes, and ensuring supporters got out to vote. It also meant leaving the air war (advertising, media, brochures, personal outreach) to others.

At the same time, I joined a club of women who did all the work but got very little credit. The candidate was always a man and the senior campaign titles were given to high-profile men in the party and the community. They would come to the office for a meeting, make the decisions and leave it to the women in the room to execute them. And we did. Maybe we grumbled a bit or rolled our eyes, but we knew we were best positioned to do the actual work. As strong, committed Liberals, what could be more important? Certainly not our individual egos.

This was the point of my career where I first learned the phrase "ivory tower." We'd joke about the men in their ivory tower calling the shots. It was an odd juxtaposition for me because at the end of the day, there was never any question in my mind who was truly in charge to make things happen. And every man involved knew that it would be a serious mistake to upset the formidable Anne Dmetriuc. If you had any ambition at all in local politics, you stayed on her good side.

Lesson: If you've found your passion, plot out the journey and don't be afraid to ask for what you want. If you don't ask, you don't get.

When David Peterson was elected leader of the Ontario Liberal Party in 1982, I was working for Liberal Member of Provincial Parliament (MPP) Herb Epp in his constituency office. He was the epitome of a middle-aged, entitled, white male politician. He was sexist and chauvinistic—he used to leave his used coffee mug in the "Out" tray, for god's sake—although he seemed unaware of it. But I was grateful for the job because I learned something new every day, and I got to do politics on the side.

At the same time, I became a Liberal volunteer organizer for the southwest, where most of the thirty-four Liberal seats were located (the caucus was often referred to as the "southwestern rump"), and I generally got my marching orders from Vince Borg, Peterson's executive assistant. During this time, I was also elected vice-president for organization for the provincial party. At twenty-four years old, my reputation as a political organizer was beginning to take shape.

In December 1983, I took three weeks away from the office and worked in a by-election in Stormont–Dundas–Glengarry, deep in the heart of eastern Ontario. We didn't have a hope in hell of winning but we wanted to send the signal that the Liberals were ready to fight for every riding. On a personal level, I wanted folks to know I was prepared to do what was needed for the party, including moving to a riding far away from home just before Christmas.

About six months later, in spring 1984, having decided to switch jobs and leave my marriage, I reached out to Vince and told him I wanted to continue working in politics—which meant either moving to Toronto or Ottawa. I gave him right of first refusal. I was thrilled when he called me back a few days later and offered me a job at Queen's Park. In that moment I knew my passion for politics would become the foundation of my professional career.

Lesson: Make your mark on a single campaign and take it from there. You don't need to be at the Centre to get noticed. Do a good job and the Centre will notice you.

With Anne, I worked provincial campaigns supporting Harry Worton in 1975, 1977 and 1981. Those campaigns did not require much work because Harry didn't really believe in spending a lot of money. He basically ran his campaign from his kitchen table and spent his time visiting farmers door to door. He won by large margins based on his solid reputation for being available to anyone in the community who needed his help. We also worked federal campaigns for Frank Maine when he was elected MP in 1974 and when he was defeated in 1979. We were thrilled to elect Jim Schroder in 1980 after Pierre Trudeau had again taken the helm of the Liberal Party. We lost in 1984.

During those campaigns, lessons came in many forms. During the federal campaign in 1984, Guelph was hosting a huge rally for John Turner, who had succeeded Pierre Trudeau as prime minister. We decided to use the public area in the downtown Eaton Centre, which turned out to be a huge mistake. I was at the back entrance waiting for Prime Minister Turner to arrive. Over the radio, a voice said, "Pat, we need you at the front of the building." Responding that I was not able to get there at that moment, they continued: "A nuclear cruise missile has just been brought in through the front doors. We don't know what to do."

I've had some strange things said to me over my years in politics but that one is near the top. Leaving the advance people to manage the prime minister's arrival, I sprinted to the front. There it was: a massive papier-mâché cruise missile being held high by a member of the Ontario Public Interest Research Group (OPIRG) whom I knew from university. He and his colleague were two of the tallest men I had seen in my life and they passed the missile back and forth effortlessly between them, holding it more than six feet in the air. Being five-foot-three, I was forced to look up at them. They smiled, looking down at me like some hobbit. I was not smiling, giving it my best effort to hector, beg and threaten—to no avail. In the end we had no choice but to bring in Prime Minister Turner through the protest. We tried to block the camera shot with balloons, but it made the nightly news. It was a tour fail and I was responsible for it. There were tough lessons that day and I've never forgotten them.

Lesson: Tough losses early in your political career teach you one thing above all others: to never take anything for granted.

I ran my first by-election, held on December 13 in 1984, in the riding of Wentworth North. The title of campaign manager was held by someone locally and I was the senior organizer assigned by the party. Despite being twenty-eight years old, I had been involved in more campaigns that anyone locally. The candidate was Chris Ward, a popular, young, up-and-coming local mayor. The seat had been held for the previous nine years by Liberal Eric Cunningham, and in theory we should have easily held the riding. However, at that time David Peterson was an unknown and the consensus of the mainstream media was that he could never win the upcoming general campaign; the Conservatives would continue to hold government for a long time to come.

It was a critical by-election. We lost by 169 votes. The loss hurt on so many levels. Seeing it as a clear message that they could continue to hold government, the smug PCs loved that the media deemed the win "Bill Davis's gold watch," given that he was retiring before the next election. There was some solace in the fact that Premier Davis never got to wear that gold watch; PC MPP Ann Sloat never took her seat in the legislature because she was defeated by Chris Ward a few months later in the May 1985 general election.

Losing the Wentworth North by-election defined my entire approach to ground organization for the rest of my career. It was an organizational failure, given the narrow margin that represented less than one vote per poll. I never pretended otherwise. I made a critical mistake that I never made again. Chris convinced me that we didn't need to pull the vote in his own backyard, the community of Troy. His neighbours and friends would be there for him and would vote. As resources were limited, I trusted his view and focused the pull elsewhere. In hindsight, if we had put an effort into pulling Liberal supporters in the area where Chris lived, we'd have won. His neighbours were no different than any other voter and we failed to get them out.

My absolute love of by-elections was ingrained from that moment forward. They became a major passion and I worked on as many of them as I possibly could. I long held the belief that every riding was worth fighting for, every election worth making the effort to win. Even if the riding was a longshot, a by-election provided the opportunity to grow the base by identifying our vote. Liberals come from all over the province to participate. We'd train people, try new approaches to reach voters and test messages about our leader.

Lesson: Take advantage of every opportunity you can find in politics—even the risky ones. Understand that some lead to success; others end in defeat. The point is to learn as much as you can and ultimately determine where your passion lies.

In 1985, with a provincial election looming, the MPP for my riding of Wellington South, Harry Worton, announced he was retiring and would not seek re-election. I had learned from him that taking care of your constituents came ahead of all else you could do in politics. Harry had won every election handily during his thirty-year career, despite the Conservative dynasty that had lasted through those same decades.

I decided to seek the Liberal nomination. I don't think I was motivated by much more than the opportunity to follow in the footsteps of an MPP I had long admired. But I also thought it was time a woman took a run. It was going to be a tough election for the Liberals, and I knew I was not the strongest option. By that point, I had overcome many hurdles as a twenty-nine-year-old woman looking to make her mark in politics. This would be one more. Local Liberals rallied around my campaign and I had help from friends with whom I worked in the party and at Queen's Park. But a last-minute entry by Guelph alderman Rick Ferraro changed the dynamic.

I lost key supporters who felt they needed to go with Rick because of his higher profile, due to his success as an elected official at the municipal level. Most damaging was losing the support of Anne Dmetriuc, who was the most influential Liberal in town and Rick's cousin. As they left, people told me they felt badly but had to support the person they felt could win the riding. I understood that sentiment. In fact, I have held that sentiment as an organizer and someone charged with recruiting candidates best positioned to win their ridings.

I placed third despite a strong presence at the nomination meeting, cheered on by supportive family, friends and local members. My parents and sisters had gone all out garnering the support of our entire extended family, even the ones who were Conservative voters.

Knowing I was on the ropes, my dad urged me to deliver a persuasive and dynamic speech. I came off the stage into my dad's embrace. Tears in his eyes, he said, "That was a hell of barnburner. Well done." Of course, the speech meant nothing to the outcome, but it is the memory of my dad I hold close.

During the nomination, my dad gave me a defining moment as a woman in politics. Just before declaring my intention to run, I had a distressing conversation with my then-husband, Jim, who was also a city alderman (I'd helped get him elected). We were separated at the time, moving toward a divorce. When he heard of my intention to seek the nomination, he asked to meet and threw me curveball. He put it to me that, as an alderman, he was better positioned to win the riding. As such he should be the one to run and I should run his campaign. I was shocked but said I'd think about it. Then came the conversation with Dad, and his reaction had a big impact on me.

Dad had been deeply disappointed by my decision to leave my marriage but, faced with the suggestion I should step back and let Jim run, he responded as a protective father would. He leaped to my defence. With some agitation, he said something like, "Why should he be the one to run and not you? You are much more qualified, and you've worked for it." And with this in mind, Dad understood the only reason I'd step aside was because Jim was a man and I was not. Not on his watch. From that point forward, Dad gave it all he had. I am pretty sure he even managed to sign up some of those union guys who had helped me as the NDP candidate in the mock student election some seventeen years earlier.

My attempt to win that nomination was a lesson in life and in politics. I learned what it was like to be on the very front line, what it took to ask people for their support, to let others organize for you. I learned that humility has two sides to it: being told yes and being told no. And no matter the answer, it is important to be grateful to have even been considered.

The experience of working with a team and fighting for an outcome is a big part of any political battle. After that defeat, I returned to my role at Queen's Park and threw myself into the general election. After we won, I realized that had I won the nomination, I would have been an MPP—but that it wasn't meant to be. I never again sought a nomination, acknowledging that my passion was in the backroom.

Lesson: In politics, you don't have to start at the top. Manage your expectations and look for opportunities to move forward, whether in opposition or government.

As VP Organization for the party, I had spent a lot of time travelling around the province working to build up local Liberal organizations. To this day people are surprised to learn I've been to virtually every little, off-the-beaten-path town they can name. After the Liberals triumphed in 1985, a lot of people wanted to be Liberal candidates. It was healthy for the party, as the membership levels increased exponentially and money poured in. Some of the local races were intense. Given my ability to control a crowd and enforce rules, I was assigned to chair many of the larger, more competitive nomination fights.

I remember a particularly tough one in the riding of Dufferin Peel, ultimately won by former cabinet minister Mavis Wilson. It was a long-held Tory riding but a good example of where we Liberals suddenly found ourselves competitive. The crowd who gathered in Orangeville was large and unruly. Many of my procedural decisions were loudly and angrily challenged, and it was taking its toll. At one point I stepped into the hallway and had a good cry. I pulled myself together and walked back into the auditorium as the vote got underway.

I noticed an elderly man moving slowly toward me. He wore an army jacket and cap and his medals were on full display. As he reached me, he said, "Young woman, I have a question for you." I braced myself for a blast. When I asked what it was, he responded, "Have you ever considered a career in the army?" I burst out laughing as he listed all of the reasons I'd be highly successful in a pressurized environment dominated by discipline and rules.

It was in those years I learned to be "bossy" in order to communicate that I was in charge. I learned that real action is on the front line. I learned that defeat and winning were two sides of the same coin when it came to campaigns. But it was always more fun, and more meaningful, to win. It was on that solid basis that I began my career in government.

My journey between ages twelve and twenty-nine grounded me in the way I would approach politics. I wound my way through its many layers and soaked in all I could from those I met along the way. There are many ways to get into politics and make an impact. I'd been a campaign worker, a riding president, a regional organizer and a campaign manager. I'd run for a Liberal nomination and lost. I'd worked federally, provincially and municipally. I'd spent four years in a constituency office learning how government works. When I finally found my way into the Centre, I was ready to make my mark.

CHAPTER 2

You Define Your Own Worth

> "I was always looking outside myself for strength and confidence,
> but it comes from within. It is there all the time."
> – ANNA FREUD

In 1985, we found ourselves unexpectedly in government after forty-two years in the "wilderness" of opposition. Ontario Liberals had long waited for this moment and much of it had to do with the announcement made on October 8, 1984, by the boring but popular premier Bill Davis. We began the day believing Premier Davis would be calling an election. Liberal staff lined the hallways at Queen's Park in an effort to demonstrate to media we were ready fight a campaign on behalf of our leader, David Peterson. We ended that day full of hope that the Liberals might have a shot, given that we would not be running against the formidable Davis, who instead announced his resignation.

After the general election the following spring, the Ontario Liberals formed government based on a Liberal–NDP Accord. We were beyond excited that the long drought had ended. I've never forgotten the feeling that washed over me as I stood on the front lawn of Queen's Park on June 26, 1985, watching the swearing-in ceremony on a hot, sunny day. I shared with others a sense of accomplishment, awe and hope. I basked in our success, thrilled I had played even a role in this moment in history.

Lesson: Understand the structure of the political environment and where you think you'd best fit in.

Every few years, voters decide who they believe best represents their interests in government. The outcome of an election determines who gets to work in politics. What is not well known is that along with elected politicians, political staff are directly tied to the government in power and if the government changes, or in some cases if the politician changes, the political staff change as well—immediately and automatically. This means that for most people, a career in politics is not an option. The exceptions are politicians who get re-elected without fail (though rarer now than it once was). Those individuals foster a base of voters who, over time, remain loyal to them no matter which way the wind blows in the larger electorate.

Political staff employed by government are public servants. They serve the public and are paid through a government or legislative payroll. However, their roles are very different from the role of the civil servant. It's often the toughest thing to get people to understand. The position is likely one of the most fascinating, exciting, fast-paced and powerful you will ever hold, but at the same time, it's one of the most unstable and demanding. It can be brutal.

When people come to me and say they want to pursue a career in politics or government, I ask them exactly what that means to them, because my response will depend on their answer to that question. In many cases, it is the desire to influence policy outcomes. In others, they have experienced politics through a campaign, often in support of a specific politician, and loved it. Many are Young Liberals who like me, joined the Liberal Party during their post-secondary education and want to spend time doing politics while they have fewer obligations and can dedicate their time to a cause they believe in. Some start as interns and become caught up in the exciting world of politics, unequaled in the outside world. Some just need a job.

I put staff who directly serve elected politicians, generally known as political staffers, into three main groups.

At the top, there is an elite group of staffers who turn their passion for politics—or sometimes a politician—into a successful career that may last a long period of time (years, even decades, although not necessarily consecutively). They excel at what they do. If their party is in government, and if they choose to be part of it, they generally have jobs. Often the way forward is that a high-performing person works with a high-performing leader or minister, or on a critical file, or both, and those circumstances allow a political staffer to rise above the pack. They must recognize an opportunity when it comes along and do what's needed to ensure a political win.

In the middle of the spectrum is the largest group—advisors who are involved for shorter terms, usually for all or part of one mandate of up to four years. They likely first volunteered because of a commitment to a specific politician or a passion for an issue, or they were recruited as a subject-matter expert or for their interest in government. Most in this group come and go relatively quickly, based on pressure from parents, spouses or others to "get a real job in the outside world" with more stability and without being ruled by the whims of the electorate.

At the other end of the spectrum are those deemed to be "hacks." They stay too long either because they can't find work outside of politics or they believe it's not an option for them. They tend to move between offices and are often attached to a single politician for a long time.

Loyalty is an important factor and an active consideration when hiring people who work directly for politicians. It is critical for a politician to have complete confidence and trust in their staff, because staffers become the face of the politician on many levels. They manage issues, provide critical advice and interact with external stakeholders. The behind-the-scenes reality is that staffers are powerful in their own rights and have direct influence on decisions made by politicians every day.

In cases where the person has not been exposed to partisan politics, I try to fully explain the precise role of political staff. People who go to work for politicians without understanding what is expected of them on the partisan side of ledger (attending party events with a politician, campaigning at subway stops or by-elections, writing political speeches) are often blindsided by what that means for their day-to-day roles. Some adapt quickly, some stay but resist it, and others soon realize that partisan life is not for them. Some stay in government but find their way into the civil service.

Lesson: Understand the value you bring and be prepared to ensure others know it, too.

Immediately after the 1985 election, I was assigned to work in the transition office and was heavily involved in staffing for new government ministers and MPPs. The location was confidential and off-site, and we worked long days in order to be ready in just a few weeks. We were given several clear mandates from Premier-Elect Peterson: first, one-third of people hired were to be from outside of the Liberal Party (stakeholders, consulting firms, subject matter experts); second, anyone who put up their hand was to be fairly considered; and finally, we were to diversify the workforce by making every effort to hire women and people from ethnocultural communities.

As all staff from the previous opposition office were assured a job somewhere in government, it was a matter of who ended up in what role. My reputation as someone who got the job done, and my extensive political experience, differentiated me from some of the newer staff. It landed me in the Centre—the Premier's Office—as the executive assistant to the executive director, Gordon Ashworth.

We needed to fill close to six hundred positions, as the existing staff base was maybe sixty people. Gordon and Hershell Ezrin as principal secretary co-led the new government on the political staff side. Hershell was the first person I'd worked with who was a senior and serious guy, in command of the day to day of the government. Gordon was the experienced, hands-on organizer I dreamed of becoming. To the external world, they worked well together. Internally there was confusion around who was running the show. It was my first experience with a workplace where internal politics impacted the day-to-day effectiveness of the organization. Unfortunately it was not to be my last.

Two years flew by quickly, as the likelihood of an election was high once the Liberal–NDP Accord came to an end. I spent most of the 1987 election driving from riding to riding checking in on local campaigns, focusing them on what was needed to ensure wins. The winds of change had taken hold and we were handed a massive majority government.

Peterson's office was led by men and there were few women at the senior staff table. David was a good old boy, and while he recognized the importance of creating more opportunity for women, it didn't apply to his own office. The most senior woman in the Premier's Office was Heather Peterson, who ran the appointment process (and some said she did not count because she was David's sister-in-law). Leading up to 1987, Deb Nash (now Matthews) was appointed campaign co-chair. I admired both women as role models and learned as much as I could from them. But I took my direction from Gordon, Hershell and Vince, who was the executive assistant to the premier.

Following the election of a majority government, I opted to leave the Premier's Office to become a chief of staff to a minister. I was honoured to be assigned to Bob Wong, the first minister of Chinese-Canadian descent anywhere in Canada and one of the kindest, most capable men I have ever met. He was quite new to the game, having just been elected an MPP.

Many were surprised I was prepared to leave the Centre. The stress on staff caused by the intense rivalry between Gordon and Hershell had taken its toll on me. After nearly four years at the Centre, I knew it was time to expand my experience and take on more responsibility—which was something not available to me at the Office of the Premier.

In negotiating my new role, I had to fight to be paid the same as men in the same position. Gordon argued with me I was too young at thirty-one to make that much money, and that the overall salary increase was too great (going from his assistant to a chief of staff). I mustered my courage and argued with Gordon that based on our government's commitment to "equal pay for work of equal value," I had to be paid the same as men in the role. And in the end, I was. It was a lesson in making the decision to push through a woman's natural tendency to "settle" rather than undergo the fight for one's worth, regardless of age or gender.

Lesson: Take the chance, speak up, wade in. But only if you have done your homework and are prepared to argue your position. Don't become known as someone who speaks just to hear their own voice.

The world had shifted, a lot. In opposition, I was part of a small but mighty group with a large challenge. In government, the change in outlook was as different as night and day. I was now one of over six hundred political staff, taking on a wide range of competing issues. The mindset was much more reactive, as opposed to taking the pro-active approach possible in opposition. Every day I had to decide where to focus my efforts.

Unlike most of the people joining government as brand-new staff, I was coming of age. For a young woman, growing up in politics had little to do with the number of years you were involved as a volunteer or a staff person. It was about the struggle to advance beyond the glass ceiling, and it wasn't easy. In a male-dominated profession, well before the #metoo movement, there was intense pressure on women both in the office and on the social scene. Young people made up the largest group of staff; most were unmarried, and many had moved to Toronto from smaller communities, as I had. There was a lot of pressure to party and accept you were going to be hit on at political events. You were called "Girl Friday," "sweetheart," "little girl," and there was an assumption you'd be the one to get the coffee.

More often than not, you were the only woman in a room of men in charge. Even if there were a few women, you were always outnumbered by the men. It was a challenge to be heard. You first had to believe you had something important to say. Then you had to find the courage to say it. You were just as likely to be ignored because of your gender than be heard because you knew your stuff. I realized the only way to gain ground was to fight to be recognized, and then push aside the tendency to be intimidated by the reaction to simply speaking up.

When I started to chair meetings later in my career, I would consciously recall that early lesson. I would look around the room at who was not speaking, trying to gauge how they felt by their facial expressions. Sometimes it was frustration at not getting a word in. That was easy to solve by inviting them to speak. If I saw discomfort or confusion, I would take a less direct approach by speaking to the issue and inviting the person to comment. Sometimes if I broke the ice by raising the other side of the debate, I would give the individual, almost always a woman, a chance to find her voice.

Lesson: You are not a girl, you are a woman. In the professional world, don't be defined by terms that diminish you.

Male staff, as well as my nephews and male friends, used to grumble about how I regularly corrected them when I heard them use the term "girls." I'd suggest they meant "women" or "young women." In some cases, tongue in cheek, I'd hear the word "girl" and ask how old the person was to whom they referred. Sometimes people would catch on right away and others would give me a straight answer. I would quickly point out that if she is over seventeen, she is not a girl.

Although aware of all the reasons it's deemed okay to call women "girls" (arguments like that's how women refer to themselves, it's meant as a friendly term, it's the norm today), I don't buy any of them. It's long been my position that in the professional world women must not refer to themselves as girls, nor should they make it okay for others to do so. The term is a reference to someone junior, or someone who isn't equal to others in the room. It's is a throwback to a day when you accepted whatever a man wanted to call you, which served to minimize your authority and maturity.

Lesson: Treat politics like a job, not a social activity. Be a professional and do the work. Get recognized by achieving outcomes, not by being a regular at the local political hangout.

As a woman making my way in politics, I pretty much put everything on the line. I knew the only way I was going to make it was to work harder and longer than everybody else. It also meant taking my disappointments in stride and accepting being passed over—something that happened many times. It meant that I'd stay the course and accept certain roles when I knew I was more qualified than the men given a more senior position. And often, I would end up doing the work of the man given that position, only to watch him take the credit.

I now tell young staff that it's about how you choose to get noticed. You can get a job as a political staffer and think the way upward is paved by attending parties and events, earning a reputation as someone who is fun to socialize with. You can hang out with politicians and senior staffers, hoping they'll remember your name the next time they see you in the hallways, or you can approach being a political staff the same way you would approach any other career: you need to make a difference. That means taking on responsibility, doing the absolute best job you can, being accountable and getting results. On that path—inevitably the lonelier one—you'll be surprised how many people will know your name.

When I started in politics, advancement was often associated with who you knew. Nepotism plays a role when politics is the family business. It dictated who got the job or the assignment and it assumed you'd perform well. What was not always clear was how closely performance was linked to popularity within the political network, which often kept a staff person in their job even if they were failing at it.

When I worked as chief of staff to minister Laurel Broten in the government of Dalton McGuinty, it was not uncommon for the Centre to assign young staff to work with me because of my expectation that they would meet performance requirements regardless of who they knew. Even if you were the son of a former MPP or labour leader, you were required to show up at work on time and do your job well. My goal was to make sure those young people came to understand their value as individuals, regardless of how they got their positions. It was said that anyone who survived their training with me could move on and do well. And they did.

I'd been in Ontario Liberal politics for about seven years prior to the arrival of the much more famous Sorbara—Greg—and his appearance on the scene brought some tension to my career. People would learn my name and ask immediately about my relationship to the finance minister (something that still happens today). Some clearly assumed I got to Queen's Park because I was related to Greg, and while it is true that he is my second cousin, we only met when I helped recruit him to run in 1985. In response to the unspoken question, I would say to people, "If you are making an assumption that my being here is somehow related to Greg, I was here first and I got *him* the job." Other times people would assume my relationship status with Greg. After I'd grown tired of it, conversations would go like this:

"I know your husband."

"I don't have a husband."

"Oh. Then your brother."

"Nope, I don't have a brother."

"Oh, I'm talking about Greg."

"Oh, you mean my father?"

"Your father??"

"Yes. Next time you talk with him, please tell him his daughter Pat says hi."

From time to time, the phone would ring and it would be Greg, who is exactly ten years older than me. He'd say, "Please stop telling people you're my daughter!" We'd laugh and I'd whine about the assumption that he was the reason I'd moved my way up the ladder.

Lesson: In politics, you end up with a reputation whether you want one or not. Make sure it's one you can live with and stand behind.

By the mid-1980s, within the inside circles of the party, my reputation as skilled, hard-driving and demanding had taken hold. And that's exactly what I was. By working on many elections and key party events, I had demonstrated my ability to lead teams and get results. When I was at the Centre, I was often the one on the other end of phone providing direction (whether it was wanted or not), giving advice (whether it was wanted or not) or chasing down political leads before they become problems.

I wasn't always happy with my reputation because, on many days, it felt more negative than positive. My only way to change that, I felt, was to settle for less from myself and others. And that just wasn't in my DNA. It often depended on the person expressing their views. Some were receptive and thrived under my coaching; others struggled and pushed back. I was willing to work with anyone who felt they could withstand my approach to leadership and my view that failure because you did not try was not an option. It was a running joke that anyone who worked with me on a by-election should earn a T-shirt with the words, "I survived a by-election with Pat Sorbara."

Eventually I learned that regardless of how I felt about it, my reputation was a fair reflection of the way I operated. The results of that intense management style got me noticed. And for a woman who had decided to compete in the fast-paced, gruelling and often unfriendly world of politics, being noticed meant opportunity.

The newly formed Peterson government faced its first by-election in 1986 in the riding of York East. Conservative MPP and former minister of labour Robert Elgie had no interest in serving in opposition following the defeat of his Conservative government. He accepted an appointment from Premier Peterson as chair of the Workers'

Compensation Board of Ontario, as it was then known (now the Workplace Safety and Insurance Board). Elgie's resignation paved the way for Peterson's first political test as a minority government, increasing the pressure for a win.

We wanted a woman candidate to demonstrate Premier Peterson's commitment to advancing the role of women in government. We recruited Christine Hart, a young, bright lawyer who lived in the riding. As she had never run before, she needed a crash course in politics, which is not abnormal in a by-election. But it was also the case that Christine was not political; she had no close political advisors to turn to with her questions and doubts. The upshot was too much second-guessing of decisions against a tight timeline by well-meaning but uninformed people who did not understand how things worked in the backroom.

I didn't get assigned to the by-election right away—I was focused on pre-writ readiness for the next general election—but Christine managed to chase away her first four campaign managers. As the by-election was about to be called, the premier was brought into the picture. His response? "Send in the bitch." A few minutes later, I was in his office and he told me I had to get in there and fix it. Although I didn't think his comment about me was very nice, I knew he meant it as a compliment. I took solace in the fact that he knew I'd be single-minded about winning.

Lesson: It's particularly true that in politics, when the going gets tough, the tough have to get going. You don't get to cut and run, you stand your ground and fight.

I liked Christine; she was a good candidate and there for the right reasons. She had pressures of her own. I quickly came to understand her family was the source of tension and the definitive factor in the departure of her first four campaign managers.

On my very first day I was sitting at my desk when Christine's brother Hugh approached me. In no uncertain terms he informed me that he considered it his job to make my life miserable. Without a word, I calmly studied him over my glasses until I could sense he was getting uncomfortable. I then advised him, in my most dismissive and firm tone, that he'd be way too busy putting up signs and canvassing to have any time to bother me. But believe me, he tried.

Christine's then-husband Rob Warren demanded a lot of input. I was prepared to give it to him on the promise he not discuss what he heard with the candidate, given that she needed to stay focused on meeting voters and not worry about campaign organization. It was quickly evident Rob was not prepared to keep that commitment, so I stopped telling him things. I could feel the pressure around the family dynamic building.

The boiling point was reached on Hugh's birthday (although I was unaware of that until after the blow up). The premier's wife, Shelley Peterson, arrived in the morning to accompany Christine to seniors' residences to seek that critical vote. They were both beautifully dressed and there was no doubt they'd be a hit with that sector. Christine told me that Hugh would be joining them for the day, which was okay with me until I saw him. He was dressed in cut-off jeans and a ragged T-shirt and when he refused to go home and change, I sent him to put up signs.

When Christine returned to the campaign office, she was furious with me, as Hugh had called her to complain. To demonstrate her unhappiness, Christine advised me she would not be campaigning anymore that day. With my frustration already pretty high, my temper boiled over. Christine was leaving out the front door and I was at the back of the campaign headquarters. Tears of anger and exasperation rolling down my face, I began to shout. I told her to go ahead and leave; if she didn't care about winning this campaign, why should the rest of us? My reaction was over the top, and it was certainly inappropriate to yell at my candidate.

But the real problem was that once in full flight, I was unable to rein in my Italian temper. I continued to shout and stamp my feet. It was unprofessional and unbecoming. My friend Bill Murray was nearby watching in disbelief. Recognizing I had lost it and was unable to pull back, he took the only action he could think of to bring the altercation to an end. Bigger and stronger, he stepped behind me, turned me around and pushed me out the back door into the pouring rain. I was instantly drenched.

Shocked and standing in the cold rain, I calmed down. Christine did not return that day. I spent the day sorting through my fatigue and the source of all that anger. I thought seriously about leaving the campaign, but I knew I couldn't do that to the party or the premier. And I wasn't going to risk a hit to my reputation by running away when the going got tough. I thanked Bill for his timely, albeit drastic, intervention. He truly could see no other way to get me to stop yelling. It turned into one of those special moments that bond people who survive the pressures of politics.

With my perspective back in place and my temper in check, the next day I apologized to Christine. We moved forward, won the by-election and remain friends to this day. This anecdote is more than a story for me. It speaks to the person I was becoming in politics. By then I had been around long enough to know there were those who saw it as a fun place to be, and those who were dedicated to the cause. It's not that the two were always mutually exclusive, as almost everyone had a commitment to the long-term health of the party. It was that I needed people to focus on the serious part when it mattered. And by-elections mattered.

Lesson: For a woman in politics, it's a fine line between being a boss and being liked.

I wanted to be a leader and I'd established my credentials as a hard worker. But I also wanted to be liked and have friends. Far too often, those two realities clashed, as politics often feels like a personality contest. The social element was extensive and far-reaching. MPPs living away from home during the week and younger staffers who were often away from home for the first time had no other place to be, so it meant they socialized frequently. It became the norm to follow the pressure-filled days with a night at the bar with friends.

An introvert by nature, I could take only so much socializing. I'd show up for the must-attends—like holiday gatherings or all-staff nights—but I rarely made it to the end of an evening. As well, when you work at the Centre and you're out for the evening, people don't often ask about how you are doing. They want to make an impression or discuss an issue or their future, which was fine with me as it made conversations easier and I was prepared to share my experience and advice. But for me, socializing in politics was not downtime.

The day after the York East by-election, Christine came by while we were clearing out the office to thank me for all I'd done to get her elected. She handed me a large bouquet of flowers, stating, "You probably don't even like flowers." I took it to mean that flowers represented the soft side of someone and she'd not seen any such side of me. I understood it but it hurt a little. And it made me think about how hard it was for a woman to be both demanding and likeable.

It was not uncommon for people unhappy with my management style to let me know that I was unpopular. I'd hear, "People would like you better if you weren't so nasty to them." It was upsetting at times, but I tried not to let it show. Usually it would happen in a stressful situation or in the lead-up to a large event, like an election or an annual meeting of the party. My response would be, "I'm not here to make friends; I have enough friends. I'm here to get the job done."

It sometimes felt like I could not have both. If I wanted to be seen as a serious person and compete for senior roles, I could not make a mistake or fail at whatever task I was handed. I regularly carried a large load between my day job in government and my political work, so I rarely had time to socialize. I was racking up wins on the political side of the ledger, but I struggled with how I was seen as a person.

It was essential to develop a thick skin. At home, I might cry or rage to manage my emotions (those who have worked with me know

I call that "kicking garbage cans"), but I tried not to show weakness in the room. Not when I was fighting my way into the big leagues. I'd journal my thoughts and feelings and occasionally talk the issues through with friends. Eventually therapy helped me sort out the triggers, put up a wall to protect myself and be indifferent to the cynics.

Lesson: It is important to back up beliefs with action. That means supporting women and finding women who will support you.

I have always tried to campaign for a woman candidate or a woman politician whenever possible. I spent the last few weeks of the 1987 general campaign in the riding of Mississauga South with Claudette MacKay-Lassonde, an engineer and the first female president of the Association of Professional Engineers of Ontario. The win was a long shot, but I nonetheless asked to work with such an amazing female candidate. The night David Peterson swept to a large majority, I stood in one of the few ridings we did not capture. We lost to Conservative incumbent Margaret Marland in a nasty fight, as Margaret did not take well to an upstart woman challenging her on several levels. We came within 599 votes.

It did not matter to me that we lost. I had been honoured to be part of the campaign, and I did all I could to get a woman elected. I took consolation in three things: David Peterson had led us to a majority government; the victor in this riding might not be a Liberal, but she was a woman; and finally, the exchange I got to witness between Claudette and Margaret on election night.

Claudette was gracious in her loss but given the nastiness, she went down swinging. At that time, the tradition was for the losing politician to show up at the headquarters of the winner to concede the election in person. It was a brutal practice but in some ways, it made sense in a day when politics was more genteel and less partisan.

The timing had been pre-arranged. When we got to the Conservative headquarters, I went in ahead to make sure things were ready to go. The atmosphere was ugly, given the big loss the Tories had suffered provincially. I was told we would have to wait, as Margaret had not yet arrived. Claudette bristled but agreed to give it a bit of time. After twenty minutes, we were about to leave when a large vehicle swerved alongside and parked in front of us. Margaret, in a floor-length, shimmery green gown, got out of the car. I sensed trouble.

Without a word, Claudette jumped out of our vehicle and strode purposefully toward Margaret. Caught off guard, I was a few seconds behind Claudette and reached them just as the handshake happened. As I registered the shock on Margaret's face, Claudette pivoted and moved quickly past me, back to our car. In asking her what she'd said to Margaret to cause that reaction, I truly feared the answer would be "fuck off." Instead, she had said, "You have won but I have lost nothing." Certainly not a traditional concession remark, but I know Claudette meant that losing the campaign did not mean defeat to her. She'd conceded nothing. To this day I carry the immense sense of pride I felt in this woman who never backed down.

In some ways, Claudette captured the attitude that should be adopted by every woman who runs. Regardless of whether you win or lose, you gain much simply by running. Your reputation is enhanced, not diminished. If you have given it your all, you have lost nothing. In fact, you will have gained an immense amount.

Lesson: Real change demands women in power at all levels, but progress has been extremely slow. It must be a priority, even when it isn't easy, to encourage women to take the leap.

Running for a nomination myself so early in my career influenced my many years of recruiting candidates. I could talk about what it was like to run and lose. As it had happened to me, it made it easier to explain that sometimes the Centre is going to look elsewhere for their preferred candidate. And at the end of day, it is the long game that is important in politics. I'd always understood that process for recruiting women was not going to be the same as the way we re-cruited men.

Recruiting women wasn't always the priority. When I first got involved provincially, we were in opposition and it was critical to re-cruit someone who could win the riding. In some cases that meant a local, middle-aged male politician with a history of electoral success was going to be preferred over a woman who was a social advocate with a strong community base.

In my early days of finding candidates, the mid-1980s, people felt politics was too rough and demanding for a woman. As importantly, women would be judged for not staying home with their children, spending several days of each week out of town. If a woman was single, she was either too young or possibly too "odd" in that voters would wonder why she was a "spinster," having not found a husband. If divorced, there must be something wrong with her, or she should be spending her time looking for a new husband.

Traditional male attitudes were only part of the problem. Often the biggest hurdle was convincing a woman to believe she should run, or that she could win. While men generally believe they have the needed experience and skills to be a successful politician, it was a tough sell when recruiting women. The belief that a male was more competent or more acceptable to the electorate was a common mis-conception. Even a woman confident enough to believe she was the best option would often feel the social pressure of the impact on her family. I rarely met a male candidate—at least not until much later in my career—who worried about that reality.

To this day, women ask many more questions about the role and the requirements to succeed. Women respond better when they understand the different elements that form life as a politician. They often love the concept of constituency work, as many are community activists at some level; the idea of having the tools to truly make a difference in a person's life is a powerful motivator.

Women ask what it will take to do a good job. How will they learn enough to contribute effectively? How will they learn about the issues, and how will they know how to vote on policy? If they have no knowledge of partisan politics, there will be many more questions about the way parties operate.

Every person who has recruited a candidate can probably share a story about meeting a couple where the husband was the potential candidate. After a few minutes, it becomes clear the woman would be the much stronger option and do a better job, for the right reasons. Many men have been motivated by the power, ego and prestige of the role. For women, it was almost always about the desire to advance an issue important to them or to their communities. I know many men who run because they want to make a difference—but in my experience it is the primary reason for women and for men it is lower on the list.

Only recently has the tide turned sufficiently to truly see more women running, supported by their spouses and families. There are not enough women elected or supported by women to make the difference in bringing fundamental change to the way politics is done and the way government operates, from within. But we are on our way.

CHAPTER 3

Never Accept That It Can't Be Done

"Luck means the hardships you have not hesitated to endure; the long nights you have devoted to your work. Luck means the appointments you have never failed to keep, the airplanes you never failed to catch."

– MARGARET CLEMENT

I had many role models during my many years working at Queen's Park but four women in particular had formidable impact on me and remain in my life to this day.

Heather Peterson was the only senior woman on staff with David Peterson. I turned to her often for advice and she'd help me work through the disappointments and keep going. I was in awe of this capable woman who understood her mandate to diversify the people who work in politics and executed this endgame against significant odds.

Kathy Robinson is the most disciplined and organized person I've likely ever known. We were Liberals together in the 1980s, and I reported to her when she was campaign chair in 1990. There was never any question who held the authority or how decisions were to be made. I turned to her often throughout my life when trouble loomed.

Deb Matthews—whom I admired from afar when she co-chaired the 1987 Peterson campaign—and I got to know each other best in the 1992 leadership contest when we both supported Lyn McLeod.

Deb's strength was understanding the big picture and building teams. She had a firm but kind guiding hand and never hesitated to speak out when she saw issues and problems.

Terrie O'Leary was a senior organizer in the 1990 Paul Martin federal leadership campaign (later becoming his chief of staff when he was appointed minister of finance). No matter when you phoned the office, Terrie was reachable. She was the only woman who could keep the men running that campaign under control. I remember wanting to be like Terrie, working day and night if that's what it took.

These were fearless, determined women who got results. I was lucky to have such amazing role models who had a direct impact on me. I learned the value of being mentored and tried to emulate them when people turned to me for support.

Lesson: Working in politics is a wildcard. Be prepared to love it or leave it.

Politics is a blood sport and it either chews you up and spits you out or it hooks you. And once hooked, there's no middle ground. It's likely to be the most exhilarating experience of your career. I truly believe there is no life like it. As much as possible, people looking to work as political staff should understand what the position entails before they take the job. A big part of it is knowing how the role is meant to work with that of the civil servant, a party representative and an elected politician. Political staff work to balance the competing needs and beliefs of each group and often play the role of mediator. The ability to search for a compromise is essential.

At the federal and provincial levels, if you work for a politician, you work for a political party. That reality can cause confusion at times. If you take a role in politics that is paid by government, including one in a legislative assembly, you will have a political role as well as a government/legislative role. Our system is based on electing a political party and as such, elected officials have political obligations.

Political staff are the ones who make sure those obligations are considered and, where possible, realized.

Among the most critical things political staff must understand is the role of civil servant who serves the government in power. Their primary responsibility is to provide politicians with their absolute best advice based on many factors including experience, research, historical context, societal impacts and financial considerations. The best advice always includes options, delineating the pros and cons of each proposal. Politicians tend to be more suspect when the civil service puts before them a single choice. As a chief of staff to a minister, I regularly sent back briefing notes or proposals because they were too narrow in scope.

One of my favourite encounters of this nature happened when I was chief of staff to Ken Black, minister of tourism and recreation. Fairly close to the 1990 election, I took a direct call from the minister of finance, Robert Nixon, who gave me clear marching orders. I was to oversee a process to ensure a significant sum of money was quickly distributed across the province. I knew from my political work we were moving toward an early election call and I understood the urgency.

I asked the deputy minister, Blair Tully, for a list of project recommendations from ministry staff. I told him the amount but asked for options to allow me to make choices. He had been around long enough to know my intent was to apply a political lens to the decisions. I had the list within a few days; it was more than one hundred pages in length. Each project was priced individually but there was no total. I decided to add up the amount of the projects listed. It was for the exact amount of money available for distribution—meaning there were no decisions for me to make. More than annoyed, I returned to the deputy's office to make the point that I had asked for a list of options but instead got only the ministry's picks.

The deputy turned to the assistant deputy minister responsible for the list and with a chuckle said, "See? I told you she wouldn't fall for it." He reached across his desk and handed me a second list— one with plenty of choices. Part of me knew I should be mad at the ministry's attempt to control the outcome, but I actually just thought it was ballsy—and clearly I had a passed a test.

Lesson: Sometimes the toughest environments are where you learn the most, but be prepared to accept your limits.

In 1990, eight years into my career, I signed up to support Paul Martin in his run for leader of the Liberal Party of Canada at the leadership convention held on June 23. I learned an immense amount during that race, and it set me up to be a lead organizer for the Lyn McLeod leadership campaign in 1991–92. The Martin leadership was an uphill battle and I gained direct experience with hand-to-hand combat in the trenches. The effort to win delegates against Jean Chrétien's formidable forces was like nothing I'd ever witnessed before.

It was during that campaign that I came to realize what it meant to challenge demanding, angry men who were set on having it their own way. You took their direction or you were slapped down. It was high risk to disagree with them, but my own Italian temper and sense of right and wrong put me in the crosshairs more often than was healthy. I was called "bitch" and "fucking dyke," told to shut up and ordered to do what I was told. I was laughed at and mocked. Through the frustration and tears I continued, unwilling to give in. But I came close to leaving a number of times.

I worked full-out and I got results, using my personal political network to win Martin delegates in ridings where it was not expected. I was earning respect, and I wanted to prove I had what it takes to operate in the trenches at that level. And I wanted Paul Martin to be prime minister.

Besides learning how to win on the front line, that campaign influenced my view of how important it was to be honest with the ground troops. Perhaps the best example was the day of the leadership vote. While we awaited the results of the first (and it turns out, only) ballot, senior organizer John Webster was speaking directly to organizers on the floor through our radios. He kept saying we had the momentum going into the second ballot and to be sure our delegates did not leave early. As I looked around the floor, it was clear we had lost. The party was organizing a row of people (called a "love tunnel," in tour terms) to guide the new leader to the stage. When I told John that over the radio, he told me to shut up and let him provide the direction. It always stayed with me that a senior organizer would expect us to ignore what we were seeing with our own eyes.

Lesson: Politics will always be there. You will be better at it if you get some experience outside of the bubble of government or partisan politics. You can come and go as opportunities are presented, but it's good to have a fallback. The instability of politics is best offset by knowing why you are there.

By some point in my early 30s, the word "hack" had begun to make its way into my subconscious, given that I'd done nothing other than politics in my career. At the same time, the all-encompassing nature of politics was taking its toll. I'd be at work no later than seven thirty every morning and I'd work all day, balancing my government day job with my political work. I rarely left before seven thirty at night and dedicated all or part of most weekends to politics. Eventually I decided a career was important to me, and the sensible thing was to make sure I had a fallback should the Liberals not win re-election.

At the time I was working with Bob Wong and he suggested I go back to school. Despite all my experience as a manager, it remains true to this day that it's tough to explain to people the skills you gain as a political staff person. With Bob's encouragement, I decided to start my MBA part-time at York University. It was demanding and difficult to balance everything but by the time we lost government in 1990, I had five courses under my belt. It was a good thing, because it opened the door to an option I likely would not have had, which was to attend Queen's University on a full-time basis and finish my MBA. I left the bubble at the end of September 1990 and spent the next few years applying all I learned in politics to life "in the real world."

My departure occurred following the defeat of the majority Liberal government of David Peterson, when we fell to Bob Rae and the NDP on September 6, 1990. It was an unexpected outcome that resulted in the only NDP government in Ontario's history, and a majority at that. David Peterson lost his home riding of London Centre to the NDP and resigned as leader that very night.

In the pre-writ and during the campaign, I worked in the central campaign as an assistant to Kathy Robinson, who was campaign chair. At her insistence I also managed the riding services package, which produced election campaign materials—signs, pamphlets and issues cards—for ridings, in an efficient and cost-effective manner. It was a lot of administrative work, but it was important.

Local campaigns always sense the ground shift ahead of the central campaign. We knew we were in trouble when ridings started to refuse material with David Peterson's photo on it, which was pretty much every piece of literature. We literally forced candidates to accept them, but there were a lot of unhappy campaigns out there when boxes and boxes of unwanted paper landed on their doorsteps.

David Peterson's sudden resignation meant the immediate trigger of the race, on an informal basis, to replace him as leader of the Ontario Liberal Party (among other reasons, having just become the official opposition, the party needed someone to act as the leader in the legislature). Since being even interim leader ensures a profile and access to resources not available to the other leadership candidates, the party and caucus insisted that the interim leader agree to not run for the permanent position. The very experienced Robert Nixon was chosen to fill the role, but he resigned that summer to take an appointment from the federal Conservative government. Following Nixon's departure, Murray Elston, a senior MPP from southwestern Ontario, was chosen to take on the interim leader responsibilities on the clear and explicit condition that he was not going to throw his hat in the ring.

It was not too long after Elston's appointment that Lyn McLeod, an MPP from Thunder Bay and former cabinet minister, announced her decision to seek the leadership. Following a call from her former chief of staff and campaign chair Bob Richardson, I met with Lyn and she asked me to join the effort. I was on my way to Queen's to finish my MBA, but I said yes. I did not know Lyn well at the time, but I knew this—if she were elected leader, Lyn would be the first woman to helm one of the three mainstream political parties in Ontario.

That mission called to me. I had been long involved in recruiting women to run for political office—and in general, getting more women to take on higher profile roles in politics, as campaign managers or presidents of local riding associations. A woman being elected leader of the Ontario Liberal Party would put a pretty major crack in that thick glass ceiling. But as the campaign ramped up, I couldn't actually contribute that much; the effort was being run out of Toronto and I was at university more than two hours away. Although it was killing me, I convinced myself I had to stay in Kingston and focus on grad school.

Lesson: Sometimes you just have to drop the gloves and fight for what you believe in, especially if it means advancement for a woman.

All that changed when Murray Elston announced he was running, breaking his commitment to stay out of the race when he was appointed interim leader. His stated reason was that he could not leave the leadership to such a weak field. That blatant arrogance and the broken commitment made me angry, but I still managed to keep my focus on my academics. After all, I had three semesters left to finish the MBA and return to the workforce. Surely to God I could stay away from politics for that long.

Wrong. I remember the phone ringing like it was yesterday. It was the landline at the place I had rented in Kingston (it would be years before cellphones became commonplace). It was late in the day and I was head down, working on a presentation due the next morning. For some reason I answered the phone. On the other end of the line was my friend Dave Gene, an experienced organizer and political staffer. He was a streetfighter who learned from some of the best in his home community of Windsor. Like me, he was a lifelong operative and proud of it.

Dave's opening comment was along the lines of, "Well, your candidate should just drop out now." When I asked why, given that Lyn was the frontrunner, Dave laughed. He stated that with Murray Elston now in the race, it was over. The province wasn't ready to elect a woman, he said, and Elston would win in a landslide. I remember having to firmly hold onto the phone, as my rage at the audacity and presumptuousness of his statement had caused my hands to shake. I pulled it together long enough to provide a generalized response through gritted teeth, along the lines of, "We'll see about that." I thanked him for the call and hung up.

I would later joke that Lyn should send Dave a thank you note for making that call. Overnight my priorities shifted. I was not about to let the first woman positioned to succeed in a leadership race be waved aside because a middle-aged Caucasian male from southwestern Ontario had broken his word and entered the race at the last minute. What's worse, he and his supporters had the nerve to believe he could win without a fight.

Refocusing my attention on Lyn's campaign meant I had to find a way to spend as much time in Toronto as I could. Scott Reid, a Young Liberal from Brockville whom I had worked with during the 1990 Paul Martin leadership, was doing his undergraduate degree at Queen's at the time and he was supporting Lyn. I approached Scott with my dilemma, and he was all in. He and I would drive into Toronto late Friday night or early on Saturday morning, returning late Sunday night. I worked full-out all weekend at my desk in the campaign office. When I could take a break from the campaign, or if I had an assignment due Monday, I did my homework at that same desk. Folks would often comment about the pile of books surrounding me (stacks of tomes in the areas of finance, statistics, international relations) as I barked out orders for the campaign. More than once during that leadership race, I silently thanked my large Italian family who had taught me the very valuable skill of holding two or three conversations at the same time.

Christmas break came, and I headed home as early as possible to aid in the race. Mark Munro, one of the young men working on the campaign, had worked with me when I was chief of staff to Ken Black at Tourism and Recreation, and he was well aware of my management style. He issued a memo to campaign staff joking that Christmas had been cancelled: Pat was coming home and there was work to do. While mostly a joke, with the delegate selection meetings taking place in mid-January and the convention happening February 7 to 9, 1992, in Hamilton, there was no time to lose. The office stayed open right through the Christmas break and anyone able to work on the campaign did so. (It also meant that I saw my family only briefly on Christmas Day and New Year's Day.)

At the end of the delegate selection meetings in mid-January, I gave Lyn a quick briefing about how the weekend had gone. In the middle of the discussion I noticed her getting a bit emotional. I realized she was quite relieved and surprised by how well we had done. It became clear to me that Lyn had prepared for the worst. I felt bad that I hadn't ever briefed her on our plan to elect as many delegates as possible. It was a moment in which I was reminded that politicians are human beings, with their own uncertainties and fears. She had let us do our work and never second-guessed us, but I could have spared her the anxiety. I was sure to provide updates going forward (and it was something I was careful to remember in every campaign I ran thereafter).

Lesson: If you are confident you have a good idea, fight to be heard. If needed, stamp your feet to force the leadership to hear you out. And if you are that leader, don't be so quick to dismiss someone fighting for your attention. They just might have an idea that can change the game.

The ground had been organized exceptionally well, with essentially a Lyn McLeod campaign manager in every riding. As importantly, we had spent a lot of time figuring out how best to work within the very complex delegate selection rules that had been put into place by the party executive. (Essentially, the number of delegates assigned to a candidate at the riding level was proportional to the percentage of the vote a candidate won in that riding. It meant you had to have enough people willing to run as delegates; otherwise you risked that a hard-won spot would be left unfilled.)

Bob Lopinski, a Liberal in his early twenties who had volunteered on the leadership campaign, had been after me for a few weekends in a row to sit down and discuss how to best work within the rules. I pushed him back more than once, citing more critical priorities. Finally, he refused to take no for an answer, and I heard him out. He had to walk me through it more than once, but I eventually realized that he'd found a way to make the rules work in our favour, given that we had the advantage of a lot of people seeking to become Lyn McLeod delegates.

We took the time to figure out which ridings would not have enough local people to fill their delegate slates—these were generally ridings where the Liberal Party did not have a strong base. We contacted the executives of those ridings and offered to submit enough out-of-riding memberships to ensure that the ratio of in-riding members to out-of-riding members was met (which in most cases was 10 percent, so for every ten local members we added one out-of-riding membership). Along with that, we made the commitment that we would not, without their express approval, run delegates who did not live in the riding.

Most ridings were grateful that we offered a way to ensure they did not get taken advantage of by campaigns willing to take their spots. As a result, when our competitors showed up on the day of the vote for the convention delegates, with the intention of adding people to the list to run, they were turned away because the out-of-riding membership quota was already full. Put more simply, if we could not have those delegate spots, no other campaign could have them either. It worked like a charm. We took some pretty angry phone calls from competing campaigns that day, but it was well worth it.

Even more importantly, Bob Lopinski's uncanny ability to figure out the angles and understand the opposition was paying off. He never again had to work to get my attention, and I've been proud to stand with him in many campaigns, such as in 2014 when he chaired the party's highly successful war room.

After delegate selection weekend, we were well in the game, which surprised many who thought Elston would catapult into the frontrunner status. The reality was that they were late into the race and we'd out-hustled them on the ground. At the same time, we were working hard to lock down ex-officio delegates who automatically earned the right to vote by virtue of their positions at the local riding level or within a provincial wing of the party.

Going into the convention, it was clear it would be a tight race. With six candidates, it was expected to take at least three ballots to get to a winner. For those who have never been to an Ontario Liberal Party leadership convention, it's a process of elimination. At the end of each ballot, the candidate last on the ballot and any candidate with less than 10 percent of the vote would be knocked out of the race; this happens until a winner emerges. The winner has to reach the 50 percent mark. Delegates are committed to their candidate on the first ballot but are free to vote for anyone on subsequent ballots.

That meant deals were being discussed. While I was privy to some of this, one of the campaign chairs, Bob Richardson, was taking the lead and I was not necessarily kept up to date on developments. To the best of my knowledge, no one had committed to coming our way once they were eliminated or had dropped out of the race. There was just too much uncertainty around who would win, so no one wanted to commit before the first ballot results were known. It would be a game-time decision.

Lesson: Keep the focus on the big picture and the brass ring. And then do what it takes to make it happen.

A few days prior to the convention, I was approached by Bill Murray, who was managing the campaign for Steven Mahoney out of Mississauga. They knew they couldn't win but wanted to place as well as possible on the first ballot. Bill and I were good friends, having worked together through the Peterson years, so I wasn't shocked when he contacted me. What was surprising was the very unusual request he asked of us.

Bill's numbers suggested that if Mahoney could pick up twenty to twenty-five votes on the first ballot, he could push ahead of Charles Beer and place fourth of the six candidates in the race. In return, Mahoney would throw his support to Lyn McLeod when he was forced from the ballot. I held my breath for a minute as the impact of the request sunk in. It was a massive opportunity to ensure momentum at the convention, which was something I knew to be essential if a win was going to be possible. But could such a high-risk strategy be implemented successfully?

I spoke first to Deb Matthews, another campaign chair, about the idea. We agreed it was wild, and it would be incredibly difficult to implement quietly. At the same time, we recognized that support from even one candidate could give us sufficient swing to win in the very competitive scenario we were facing. So, we decided to take it up the chain of command. Together Deb and I approached Bob. I recall one or two others in the room, but I don't remember who they were. The answer was no—we could not take the risk. It was Bob's view that we needed all our support with us from the first ballot; otherwise, we could inadvertently miscount and hurt our chances by letting Elston get too far ahead too early on.

I knew in my gut it was the wrong decision. I went back to my data and checked our numbers again, for what felt like the millionth time. I trusted the data and I believed it accurately forecasted what would happen, ballot by ballot. I went back to Deb and said exactly this, and ultimately we decided to go ahead on our own. It was not meant to be disrespectful or deceitful, but we knew there was no choice; we had to do what would give us the best chance to win the leadership. With such a large number of ex-officio delegates, it was easy to identify twenty-five people we could trust to do what was needed without asking a lot of questions.

The Friday evening prior to Saturday's balloting, Deb and I reached out to the individuals identified and explained the situation one by one. These had to be people with ex-officio status because under the rules, elected delegates were bound on their first vote. Reactions varied. Some were intrigued, some thought we'd lost our minds. (A few said no, they just couldn't do it.) We finally convinced enough delegates to do as we asked on the basis that it was for one ballot only, and that the reward was well worth the risk. We sealed the deal with Bill. Shockingly, not one word leaked overnight.

It was indeed worth the gamble. However the extra twenty-five votes ended up keeping Mahoney from finishing last, but he was only twenty votes ahead of David Ramsay so he was sitting in fifth rather than fourth. A furious Bill Murray accused me of reneging on the deal. Bill and I had a heated exchange at the back of the balloting area. I gave him a partial list of the individuals we had asked to vote for Steve and urged him to check with them on how they had voted. I also explained as calmly as I could that our numbers always showed Beer solidly in fourth place, and that the votes we loaned to them likely wouldn't have allowed Mahoney to overtake him.

Our actions actually pushed Ramsay to last place, allowing Mahoney to finish fifth. I further explained to Bill my belief that some of Steve's ex-officio support had bled to Greg Sorbara, who had entered the race late—something Bill admitted was likely true. He eventually calmed down and the deal remained intact. After the second ballot, Steve Mahoney kept his promise to cross the floor and throw his support to Lyn McLeod. It was a game-changer, as we were able to show momentum and grow our vote. I'll never forget the look on Murray Elston's face, watching helplessly as Steve Mahoney turned into our candidate box.

Lesson: The ground game matters. Don't let anyone tell you otherwise.

When I look back on the 1992 leadership convention, I recall that we ran the day with military discipline and precision: I had fought to get radios for fifty people, despite being told the budget allowed only twenty-five. I said it was not enough to cover the ground. There would be no air war that mattered that day. The outcome would be dictated by tracking each delegate as their candidate dropped from the race. Only brute force would make that possible, which meant literally tracking people for twelve hours across Copps Coliseum and several surrounding hotels and restaurants (today there would likely be an app for it!).

There were probably two hundred people working the delegates, reporting to the fifty people on the radios. It was a manual effort—it was labour intensive and required incredible attention to detail. I had carefully hand-picked each person carrying a radio based on my belief that they would stay focused and not be distracted by the social part of the convention. And if I did not hear from them at least hourly, I went looking for them.

I had been relentless around keeping Lyn focused on talking to delegates. When a candidate freed their delegates, which they all did except Steve Mahoney, we needed Lyn to speak with as many of them as possible. The problem was that what little time was available between ballots was peak time for media. There was a critical moment where I needed Lyn to convince a delegate to vote for her. I found her in a media scrum and was told I'd have to wait. In my mind, that was not an option. No one who mattered to the outcome was watching television. I literally reached in and physically yanked Lyn from the scrum. It was not well-received by the media or our communications team, but I was wholly focused on whatever it took to bring over one more delegate.

One of most extraordinary and intense moments I've experienced in politics was after Greg Sorbara left the ballot. If he threw his support, he'd decide who would be leader (the usual reference was "king-maker" but there was a woman in this race). No one knew what he planned to do. As soon as the fourth ballot results were announced, I headed over to Greg's candidate box. I could see him from the floor but we were warned to stay out while he consulted with his team and made his decision. I headed back to our box and decided to try to phone him from the landline installed there. I had carried around a small, laminated card in my pocket all day and I took it out for the first time. On the card were the numbers for the landlines in each candidate box—all except the one I needed. It was the first time that day that our attention to detail had failed us.

Time was running out and I was running on adrenaline. It was midnight by now, and we'd been on the convention floor since noon. I stood on a chair in order to be seen and yelled to anyone who could hear me to "Get me the fucking number." A few seconds later I heard Steve Hastings, one of our organizers, yelling my name. I looked over at him and he threw me a roll of masking tape. Exasperated, I yelled that I did not need masking tape. But I managed to catch the roll and something caught my eye. Steve had written the number around the outside of the roll, as he didn't have any paper. Shaking my head at the absurdity of it all, I dialled the number.

Isobel Finnerty, Greg's campaign chair, answered the phone. She and I were not on the best of terms but I had learned a lot from her when we worked together in the Premier's Office and we respected each other as political operatives. She would not let me speak to Greg as he was about to address his delegates. Then she did something she did not have to do, and it was pretty special.

She put the phone down but left the line open so I could hear Greg's speech (with the added benefit of blocking anyone else trying to get through). His speech was emotional and moving. My heart soared as I heard him free his delegates. The minute he finished I signalled to Lyn and our assembled team to rush en masse across the bleachers to Greg's area. Our system kicked in and with discipline and laser-focus, we reached out to as many delegates as we could before the final vote commenced.

I caught Greg's eye but I could tell he did not want to talk with me. It wasn't the time and he'd done what he believed was best. He and I talked about it many times in the years that followed, and he'd remind me that his decision to release his delegates made it possible for us to win. He was right. Had he thrown his support to Elston, his very committed delegates would have followed him and we would have lost. Many of his delegates left without voting on the final ballot and others spoiled their ballots by writing in Greg's name.

In the end, it came down to nine votes. There is no doubt in my mind that our organizational efforts won the day. (The only blip I remember is that damn laminated card.) I believe it is the closest delegated convention in history. And when the convention ran seriously over the scheduled timing, we placed volunteers at the doors to try to prevent delegates from leaving before the final ballot. Many did leave, but we worked to ensure as few of them as possible were Lyn McLeod voters.

We knew every single vote was going to matter. (As an aside, I remember that the convention was held shortly after a well-known Liberal strategist named Rick Anderson had left the federal Liberal party and joined the federal Reform party with Preston Manning. He had been elected a Lyn McLeod delegate and when he asked me if he should still attend the convention, I said yes, we would need every single vote. I remember walking by him in the stands and putting my hand on his shoulder. We exchanged nods and he knew I was grateful that he had come to support Lyn, despite some of the personal discomfort he was experiencing as a result of comments about his defection to Manning. I overheard him say to one person, "I am still an Ontario Liberal, whether or not that's okay with you.")

It sure was an amazing moment when MPP Mavis Wilson turned around at two a.m., after twelve hours and five ballots, flashed me a big smile and held up nine fingers. In exhaustion, I mouthed, "We won by ninety?" She shook her head, still smiling and showed me the nine fingers again, representing the nine votes. When it was officially announced, Dominic Agostino—who would go on to become an MPP for Hamilton East and to die far too young in 2004—enveloped me in a bear hug as the place erupted into cheers. I will admit I took a moment to glance over to the Elston box, and specifically at Dave Gene. I truly felt for them, knowing it's a tough way to lose, but inside I was overjoyed that our hard work and refusal to give up carried us over the finish line. I'll bet Dave was sorry he ever called me.

Precision made it possible to be on the right side of a tight result. It was a lovely moment to walk back into our campaign office to chants of "Pat, Pat, Pat!"

When it was all said and done, exhausted delegates who had lasted until the end headed home or back to their hotels. Excited workers wanted to celebrate despite it being the middle of the night, and the fact that some of us had been up for almost forty-eight hours. It was only then that I realized we had not planned a victory party; we had only planned to win. Several of our guys went to the Elston suite, which was empty of people but had a lot of beer up for grabs. The beer was brought over to our suites and an exhausted but exhilarated group held a small celebration. I said I was going to try to drink nine beers in honour of the nine votes. I recall I was nursing beer number four when I gave into the exhaustion and went to bed.

In hindsight, I've always had this thing about planning victory parties. I have very few superstitions in politics but planning a victory party is one of them. In campaigns I manage, I never take part in it and I don't allow it to be discussed in my presence.

To this day, Bob and I have never discussed that we'd gone against his decision. In fact, nothing was revealed for years, despite the number of people involved. Any murmurings were set aside as rumours. The actual details went into the vaults of those who were in the know, and there was no value in bragging about it or having the story hit the streets. The value was in taking the calculated risk to bring about the greater likelihood of the win, not about being able to take credit for it.

Lesson: Politics will push you to your limits. Go there, then go a step farther and use the moment to learn more about yourself.

During the Lyn McLeod leadership campaign, there was an incredible amount of effort put into ensuring we had a plan ready for every situation that might present itself on the day of the vote. Much of that depended on the tracking of each individual delegate and their voting plans based on the ballot-by-ballot decisions. There was a moment when all of that hung in the balance. I knew the outcome we needed, and I had to make someone cry to get to it.

When I got to the suite where staff gathered to celebrate, campaign co-chair Tim Murphy looked at me and said, "So how many people did you make cry today?" I remember, to this day, how crushed I felt by that remark. My euphoria over the win crashed immediately. Bob Lopinski jumped in and talked about the magnificent win, but the comment had hit its mark and taken its toll on me. Tim was joking at the expense of my reputation as a hard-driving, take-no-prisoners organizer, but it was not the nicest thing to have thrown at me in the context of the incredible feat we had just achieved. We had elected the first woman to lead a major political party in the province of Ontario, and it was the Liberal Party.

Had I answered Tim's question honestly, I would have admitted to making at least one person cry. Reema Khawja was a young woman in her early twenties and a wizard with data. Together we had developed a tracking system that integrated the data collected over several weeks of canvassing delegates. It was the basis on which decisions had been made to date and would dictate our approach on the convention floor the next day. We had a buddy system organized that ensured we knew who to target based on the outcome of the previous ballot. At whatever point a delegate indicated they would give their support to McLeod, someone from the campaign needed to be standing by their side. It was a massive endeavour and much more manual than could ever be considered efficient. But it needed to be done so we used the only tools available to us: tracking and the brute-force ground game.

Late Friday night we discovered an issue with the data we would be using to direct the ground troops. I don't remember it being major but it was enough to make me doubt the information we had was as correct as it could be. I asked Reema what it would take to fix the problem. She explained it was straightforward but laborious and in fact could take several hours. Reema was exhausted and argued we could manage without the fix. Maybe we could have, but it meant hitting the convention floor the next day without perfect data. Knowing how tight the race was going to be and that every vote would count, for me that just wasn't happening.

Following a bit of a shouting match, Reema began to cry, saying she just needed to go to bed. I responded by acknowledging that she was exhausted and she had every right to go to bed, but before she did she needed to show us how to fix the data. I had at least twenty people there ready to get the fix done. Reema was proud of what she had created and owned it. Once we both calmed down and she understood the fix was happening one way or another, she gave us lessons and stayed until it was finished. I have never felt more confident of data than I did with the binder of information I was handed the next morning.

After the win, Reema came to me and thanked me for pushing her past the point of wanting to quit. She had no way of knowing how critical her efforts would be in such a tight race. Winning by nine votes meant your data was precise and the massive ground effort was executed as perfectly as possible. Reema deserved much of the credit for the outcome of that day. Was a short moment of conflict and the tears worth it? You bet. In hindsight, would we have traded that outcome for a few extra hours of sleep? No way.

If Tim had asked me, I would have admitted that I had cried that day, too, several times. The pressure had been overwhelming. As the convention got underway, I stood in the rafters of Copps Coliseum and absorbed the impact of the mass of people gathering on the floor below. I promptly turned around, went into the ladies' room and threw up. I straightened myself up, looked in the mirror and ordered myself to pull it together. Today we'd call it "getting your game face on." I would do all I could to lead the group to victory. Nerves were not my friend but adrenaline, and confidence in the plan and the team, made the difference in getting through.

For a young woman working her way up the ranks and advancing a career, there were many moments of having to push through tears and focus on the task. Some of those moments defined me and taught me that I could get through it no matter what. Those lessons became ingrained and gave me a sense of self I could trust and believe in.

CHAPTER 4

Mediocrity Is Not an Option

> "Women are always being tested... but ultimately, each of us has to define who we are individually and then do the very best job we can to grow into that."
> – HILLARY RODHAM CLINTON

Following the 1992 leadership campaign, I returned to Queen's University and finished my MBA. Although I likely could have picked up where I left off at Queen's Park, I was determined to get a job in the private sector. I joined Superior Propane as the manager of government relations. I took a $10,000 pay cut from my last position in politics. When I quickly showed my value to the corporation, I made it up within a year, getting a salary increase associated with a promotion and an annual bonus based on job performance.

Political staff at Queen's Park are well paid at most levels and that's partly why it is tough for people to leave. It remains the norm that a similar role in the private sector (and certainly at a non-governmental organization) are lower paid. I still encourage people to make the leap, saying that once you prove your worth you are likely to quickly move up the line both in terms of position and pay scale.

Despite many challenges, I used the experience to learn as much as I could about how the private sector differentiated from government and the wider public sector. Sadly, I also learned early lessons about workplace harassment (and what would today fall into the #metoo movement). I stuck it out for almost three years, determined to earn my credentials in the private sector. When I couldn't handle it a minute more, I resigned on a Saturday, with no notice period, just to make the point that I'd spent most weekends at the office with very little acknowledgement of how hard I worked for that organization. As well, with a provincial election looming, there was an obvious option for me.

In early 1995, I took a job in the Office of the Leader of the Opposition and focused on the goal of getting Lyn McLeod elected the first woman premier of Ontario. It was widely expected the Liberals would win the 1995 provincial election. Perhaps that's why throughout the campaign it felt like we were coasting. What alarmed me most was what happened when the numbers began to slide. There was no plan B. The leadership had assumed the campaign would roll out exactly as they had planned. When the ground shifted under our feet, no alternatives had been worked up to allow us to quickly alter the air war in order to respond to several forced errors.

Voters keen to be rid of Bob Rae and his "Rae Days" bypassed the Liberals and landed solidly in the world of Mike Harris and his "Common Sense Revolution." On June 8, 1995, the Conservatives were handed a huge majority government. Liberals lost seats but remained the official opposition.

Most of the opposition staff, including Lyn's chief of staff Bob Richardson, left soon after the election. Disappointed we had not formed government, and being at least four years until the next election, many felt it best to pursue other options. I couldn't blame them. Lyn had been re-elected by her riding but decided to resign as leader a few months after the election. She agreed to stay in the role until a new leader was chosen. It was assumed it would be a short period of time, but the leadership convention did not take place until December 1996, a full eighteen months later.

Lesson: Often circumstances dictate your options. You still give it your all, but sometimes the scale will tip towards the personal over the professional.

I decided to stay, and was moved into the role of chief of staff. I wanted Lyn to feel supported and have some continuity among her team. It had been incredibly tough on her to lose the election and have most of her staff move on. At the same time, my personal reality made it difficult for me to make a career change.

Three years prior, my dad was diagnosed with prostate cancer. It had already metastasized so we understood the horrible disease would ultimately take his life. He was determined to fight for as much time as he could get and to do that, he needed his family. Between 1992 and his death on December 29, 1996, I was back and forth to Guelph on a regular basis. I joined my dad and mom and my sister Vikki for his treatments and doctors' appointments, many of them in Hamilton. I was undergoing intense psychotherapy at the time and the two did not make for an easy road.

My role at Queen's Park allowed me the flexible schedule I needed to manage my circumstances. We worked hard and Lyn was fully committed, but public expectations were low around how the Liberal caucus would perform as we awaited the selection of a new leader. I encouraged staff to take as much vacation as they could and to think about their futures. In the summers, departments covered off for each other to allow teams to take a weekly golf day. It remains my view that staff rarely get downtime in politics, so when it's available you take it.

Dalton McGuinty was elected leader on December 1, 1996, at a delegated convention, by a narrow margin on the fifth ballot. I stayed until early January to oversee his transition. Dalton was very understanding and kindly gave me as much time away from the office as I needed. On the afternoon that Dad died, my cell phone rang. It was Dalton calling to offer his condolences. I'll never forget how he took time away from the Christmas break with his family to personally reach out and let me know he was thinking of me and my family.

I left Queen's Park for the second time in January 1997, as Dalton's team moved quickly into place. They no longer needed me, but they did need my office. I took a few months off to start to recover from Dad's death and to work out the next step in my career. I decided to do some consulting while I figured it out. The one thing I did know was that I needed a break from the intensity of politics—at least for a year or two.

Lesson: Opportunity shows up in the strangest places. Despite the task at hand, look up from time to time to see what's out there. You don't have to act on every possibility but learn to recognize one when you see it.

Out of the blue in the spring of 1997, I had a call from two friends, Steve Hammond and Phil Playfair, who had gone into business together. Steve, Phil and I had met during the McLeod leadership. Steve had founded a utility billing and customer service software company called Advanced Utility Systems Inc. and he'd hired Phil to help him market the new software to potential clients. Phil was well aware of my management style and convinced Steve I could help them get the company off the ground. Like almost all other opportunities I was to find along the way, there was a need for someone to ensure the trains ran on time. I couldn't see it being a long-term career step for me, but I was keen to support my friends.

Critically, I knew next to nothing about software, but I was anxious to use my organizational skills and my MBA to see if I could make a difference. It turned into a daunting but exhilarating adventure, and one that taught me many lessons, personally and professionally. Despite my best intentions to establish the operational side of things and then move along, within six months I was the CEO and a shareholder of the newly formed Advanced Utility Systems Corporation.

Lesson: The skills you learned in politics are transferable to any role you take on in the future. They are the exact skills needed to excel no matter where you work. Know they will serve you well.

While I intuitively knew the skills learned in politics would be extremely valuable in the private sector, it was in working at Advanced that I came to recognize just how valuable. Every staff member we ever hired was carefully chosen. I looked for certain characteristics and personality traits in whomever I hired. When you run your own company, mistakes have to be quickly addressed or performance and finances are impacted.

At the top of my list of requirements was work ethic. I had long said to political staff that I could teach them about a product or a company, but I could not teach them work ethic. My experience at Advanced reinforced that belief. When I eventually returned to politics, I would talk often with staff about jobs in the private sector. So many young staff felt concerned they would never be able to get a job in the "real world." I would make every effort to convince them that in fact, they already had skills that most prospective employees did not. Along with work ethic, those skills included managing priorities, multi-tasking, being able to sort through a lot of complex material to create a two-page briefing note and always keeping an eye on the long game.

It was essentially second nature to model software implementations after campaigns. The date the client needed to be live on the software was our election day. From there, we created a workback plan and held daily meetings to assess our progress. It felt like running several local campaigns during the same general election. If something or someone fell through the cracks in one of those campaigns, we would fail. And failure was not an option. Like campaigns, we went into each day ready to kick ass and deal with whatever the world threw our way. We continued to grow and by the end of our nine years together, we had around ninety staff and over one hundred clients across North America and the Caribbean.

Lesson: You can learn a lot by working for a demanding boss and by surviving a challenging environment. If you can't get out of it, get into it.

Most staff came to realize that after working with me, they were well-positioned to survive a demanding boss no matter where they were employed. They might have disliked the pressure at the time, but any high-performing employee is better off knowing how to deal with it. Staff around me realized they could count on me to provide feedback and direction whether they wanted it or not. Or if they were confused by a task, they could seek clarification from me. For some, it was the first time in their lives they'd experienced real and honest feedback about how effective they were at their jobs.

I tried to demonstrate my appreciation as often as I expressed frustration, but I'll admit I wasn't always successful. The reality is that when issues arose, my state of mind was rarely taken into consideration. It wasn't usually an option to talk about the pressure I was facing or about the issues I knew about but could not mention. I found staff expected me to always manage my emotions and my reactions to problems. It was just not that straightforward—sometimes the pressure got to me. And in those times, I found myself less able to manage my anxiety and irritation.

Having said that, if someone was failing to meet their obligations and it impacted the outcome of a project, I admit I was relentless about it. I tried to always make my expectations clear: "You always know where you stand with Pat Sorbara" was commonly heard. I knew I made staff nervous. When I talked to friends about it—friends who knew politics—some argued it was a good thing to have staff be a little bit afraid of you. It meant they didn't disregard your direction or fail to do the assigned task. It meant they could feel good about their efforts, particularly when an overall objective was achieved.

Staff also came to realize I did not respond well to surprises. I wanted to be told about issues as they arose and kept up to date on files. I taught staff how to decide when to just proceed, when to wait for approval and when to escalate. When I trusted a person, they got a lot more leeway than the person I didn't know well or had had performance issues with in the past. If I could teach a staff person only one thing, it would be to do their absolute best; to do everything required to produce the desired outcome even if it meant working several late nights in a row, putting business ahead of play and focusing on the deadlines. I didn't require perfection, but I required their best.

By 2005 I was at a crossroads. I never felt Advanced was my life's work. Physically and emotionally I was exhausted, and I could no longer see the future. I was turning fifty in 2006 and I knew it was time to move on. After considerable anguish, Steve, Phil and I made the decision to sell our company. I was deeply concerned about how clients and staff would manage but I was convinced by friends and family that it was finally time to put myself ahead of others. I was always happy that we sold to a Canadian competitor who kept many of the staff in their roles. Advanced was a success story, and on a personal level I learned about a part of me I never knew could thrive. I applied every skill and technique I had learned through politics and let my work ethic take it from there.

Lesson: Sometimes it's necessary to drop everything and manage a crisis. Knowing when that is the case will serve you well.

In mid-2006, I was asked to take on the role of convention returning officer for the federal Liberal leadership contest held in Montreal. I was both honoured and terrified when party president Mike Eizenga made the request. Despite my determination to take a break after my major career change, I was drawn toward this one-time opportunity to take on a leadership role at such a significant event for the party, and at the national level.

It was a wild ride, and one I had to approach from an angle different than my norm. I was required to be neutral and apply the rules fairly across all campaigns. I was responsible for leading the team that would ensure an efficient process to register delegates and administer the vote. I would have the final decision on matters under dispute. Simply put, my whole job was to enforce the rules, ensure a fair vote and do so while controlling the chaos brought about by six thousand voting delegates and an overall attendance of ten thousand people. And with eight people vying for the leadership (Scott Brison, Stéphane Dion, Ken Dryden, Martha Hall Findlay, Michael Ignatieff, Gerard Kennedy, Bob Rae and Joe Volpe), the competition was intense.

With a large contingent of staff and volunteers, I was grateful that my friend Christine Hampson had accepted the job of deputy convention returning officer. Beyond all else that she took care of, it was her attention to detail that ensured one major disaster was derailed before anyone knew about it. Delegates were bound on the first ballot, which meant they were required to cast their vote for the person they had been elected by their ridings to support; only ex-officio delegates had an open ballot.

The usual practice and the one I had authorized was that delegates were given a coloured ballot based on the candidate to which they had attached themselves. That meant there could be no confusion around the vote or any chance of anyone trying to change their first ballot support; delegates were given their coloured ballot (with only the name of their candidate on it) by the deputy returning officer and they deposited it directly into the ballot box, without having to mark it. Ex-officio and independent delegates would vote on a regular ballot with all candidates listed. All ballots were counted, as not everyone cast a first ballot.

The day before the vote, Christine let me know she was going to check the boxes of ballots, which had been stored in a secure area. I assumed she was checking to ensure there were enough ballots to get us through several rounds of voting. Not long after, she was back on the convention floor. I looked up to find her standing in front of me. She said, "I don't know what you're dealing with right now, but it cannot possibly be more important than what I need to tell you." Based on those ominous words and the look on her face, I immediately moved with her to a quiet area.

Something, likely the intuition of someone who had been a returning officer for hundreds of riding nomination meetings, made

Christine decide to open up every single one of the many boxes that had been delivered from the printer. She informed me that there were no coloured first ballots among them. It appears they had not been printed. Once I recovered from the shock, we pulled in Steve MacKinnon, the national director of the party. He confirmed that a decision had been made to have the deputy returning officers mark each ballot on behalf of the voter. That meant the time required to complete the first ballot would be much longer than anticipated but more importantly, it meant a higher likelihood of error.

The change had been made without my approval or knowledge, and it was not what I had discussed with the official agents for each of the candidates. It represented a clear and present danger to the outcome of the convention, and it was never going to fly. It was most impressive to watch Christine take command of the situation. She told me to focus on the urgent matters I was already facing down, and she would take care of the ballot issue. With the help of local volunteers who were kept in the dark about why one was needed, she located a printer. And by some miracle, that printer agreed to produce the needed ballots within twenty-four hours.

Our next fear was that the issue would leak, which is why the printer was so carefully selected. (A funny moment came when the only comment the printer had was about the colour of Ken Dryden's ballot. She felt strongly that, after all his years playing for the Montreal Canadiens, his ballot should be red, white or blue. As I recall, we did our best to accommodate her.) Once underway, the first ballot went off without a hitch. At the end of it, Christine and I exchanged knowing glances. Our mandate to ensure the veracity of the vote had been met.

After all was said and done, the Liberals elected Stéphane Dion as our new leader, leaving the supporters of front-runners Michael Ignatieff and Bob Rae in a state of shock.

Lesson: If you work as political staff, you are a partisan and the needs of the party are a priority.

Working to be true to its values does not make a government partisan. Any decision that might impact a government's chance of re-election is fair game. It's why all decisions are looked at through the political lens. It's why some policy initiatives are highlighted in the public and others are not. And it's why the control of the narrative around a decision is critically important. If you're not in control of what's being said about your government, it hurts your brand and your chances of being re-elected.

There are some who think re-election should never be a factor, but I'm not one of those people. If you believe in what your government is doing, you should want to continue. To continue, you have to be re-elected. It seems so simple from the inside, but it's a difficult concept to communicate. I shake my head when I hear pundits demand better of government because they are the government, yet they tend to ignore partisan action by the opposition. It's a simple fact that for as long as we have a party system, action will be taken in the context of whether or not it will make a difference in the next election.

In the microcosm of a by-election, the process is more obvious. As soon as it's clear there might be a by-election in a riding, the riding goes on "by-election watch." This means all decisions related to that riding are vetted through the Centre. Nothing happens on a file unless it's been reviewed by the one person assigned by the Centre to decide what goes forward and what is held. It can be as simple as holding off on an appointment or announcement, or it can be ensuring a local irritant is resolved as quickly as possible.

The party is the only entity free to act in a fully partisan nature. Its staff interact with political staff to ensure messaging is consistent and goals are met. This is particularly evident around communications and outreach to the party membership and the general public, whether it be in the form of voter persuasion, fundraising or building up the brand. Party members expect to be kept up to date on the work of the government.

Political staff, along with riding volunteers, are the workforce of a party. This is true if you're in government or opposition. It's just much bigger if you are in government. Wearing their partisan hats, staffers work on elections, help out at nomination meetings, assist with fundraising and attend partisan events. In my opinion, it is in the partisan work where the team finds its spirit and lifelong friendships are cemented. This is particularly true when staff take a leave or vacation for several weeks to work on a by-election, special project or a general campaign. The intensity that surrounds a small group working to ensure a win for the party can be life-changing.

My friendship with Peter Donolo is an example of how working together on a short-term but intense political project can change a relationship. I'd known Peter for a long time and we always said hello, but that's as far as it went. But he called me in 2009 and invited me to lunch at his favourite restaurant, Terroni. He told me he had agreed to go to Ottawa to serve as chief of staff to the federal leader of the opposition, Michael Ignatieff. Ignatieff's efforts to break through were failing and he had decided to change up his senior team.

Peter's good friend Chaviva Hosek encouraged him to accept the role but reminded him he'd need someone to run the trains. Peter's strength is vision and overall strategic planning and communications. He decided I was that person and offered me the position of chief operating officer. After thinking about it for a few weeks, I agreed to go. It had been a few years since we sold Advanced and I was ready to get back in the game. But it was the opportunity to work with Peter that got me to the decision to re-enter politics on a full-time basis.

When I look back on that time, what I remember most is the incredible team we were able to put in place—a team that gave their all. But what I'm most grateful for is the enduring friendship I established with Peter and with his family. We've stood together through some difficult moments and frustrating outcomes. I didn't see that friendship coming, but to this day it forms a meaningful part of my life.

Peter's invitation was a call to action, and I took it. And while most staff embrace this kind of opportunity, some resist and do only the minimum required. It can be career-limiting because it can appear you aren't committed to the overall imperative of the organization, and it is on party leadership to help staff understand that side of their jobs and ensure the line between the political and the partisan is understood and respected. In opposition, it's almost always a requirement of being a political staffer. After decades in politics I have learned this certainty: political staff are the backbone of any party. During campaigns, their lives are put on hold as they commit fully to election efforts. They travel with elected officials and after events end, they go back to their rooms to answer emails, return phone calls and read policy documents.

Lesson: Be who you are and don't worry about the labels. Building others up does not diminish you; it makes you a better person.

Despite years of volunteering at the federal party level, I'd never been employed by the federal Liberals or federal government, or even in Ottawa, until Peter asked me to join him at the Office of the Leader of the Opposition. It was exciting to take up temporary residence in the nation's capital, a city I'd visited often and had come to love.

I remember the first day, standing in front of the people still employed after Ignatieff had made a series of changes to his staff. Peter introduced the new leadership team he had assembled, and I stood proudly among them. I imagined how the staff felt as they sat there looking at their new bosses, at those who would determine the road ahead. I'm sure some had hope and others, closely attached to the previous leadership, were upset and unsure of the future. We had our work cut out for us. It was a minority government and an election could be triggered at any time. We needed to focus both on being a strong opposition and on election readiness.

My title was chief operating officer reporting directly to Peter as chief of staff. I ran the day to day; all staff reported to me except for the principal secretary. With the number of changes in personnel, in some ways we were starting from scratch. I established much needed processes and protocols. Peter and I were thrilled with the way the team ultimately came together—functionally strong, united and focused on the goal of defeating Stephen Harper and his Conservatives.

I often joked with Peter that he got me there under false pretences, saying I'd have a manageable schedule that would allow me to get home to Toronto on many weekends. Finding myself working full-out on government, party and pre-writ campaign readiness, I threatened Peter that I was going to unfurl a banner from the Peace Tower that read, *Peter Donolo is a big fat liar.* Despite the pressures, I found myself loving every minute of it. Working with Peter was a career highlight for me (partly because he can pun his way out of any situation).

The production and execution of the road show known as "the Liberal Express" was the pinnacle of our time in Ottawa. In an effort to move voters in our direction, we decided to put the leader out on the road for about three months, doing a combination of government events (town halls, outreach to key stakeholders and multicultural groups) and as many Liberal Party events as we could squeeze in, including whistle stops (usually at a Tim Hortons). Talk about a high-risk strategy.

The Liberal Express was designed as both a small-scale air war and a massive ground effort, and it had the side benefit of collecting data. The project was branded, and media was a key component of each day. We outfitted and wrapped a bus and took to the road (we flew the longer distances), giving Michael and his wife, Zsuzsanna Zsohar, a real-life understanding of what the campaign would be like. In the next general campaign there would be no room for error, so the practice session served many purposes. Each day while the Liberal Express was operating, the planning team would review a literal minute-by-minute itinerary for the coming days—just as we would in a campaign.

At the kickoff event in Ottawa, I was warned by Gordon Ashworth, the campaign chair, not to call it a rally. When I asked him why, he said we shouldn't set ourselves up for failure right out of the gate. I agreed that we needed to get it right from the beginning but to do that, we needed a high-energy event overflowing with people (otherwise known as a rally). I decided to take the risk. Using the then-new technology known as robocalls to invite the general public and pulling every available staff member and Ottawa-area Liberal and their families, we filled the place to the rafters. It was a highly successful kickoff.

What was not so successful was when the bus broke down on the way to its first event in Cornwall. I thought staff were playing a joke on me when they called me from the road to say the bus driver had to pull over and that it looked bad. I made a panicked call to Gordon, whose direction helped me quickly put into place a backup plan, moving the tour vehicles into place to move the leader and the media to the event while everyone else remained until the replacement bus arrived. The Cornwall crowd had waited for the leader; we had the Express fixed for the media to board the next morning. We were able to treat it as a bump in the road, but it was a near-miss. By the end of the tour, we'd reached thousands of Canadians. The Liberal Express delivered what we needed—momentum, a leader better prepared for primetime and a demonstration to the media that the Liberals were in the game.

In March 2011, an article (sadly entitled "Flatlined") appeared in *Maclean's* magazine. Paul Wells interviewed Peter Donolo about our work in opposition and how we might fare in the upcoming election. During the interview, Paul made the point to Peter that he'd heard from some that it was in fact Pat Sorbara who ran the Leader's Office. Peter was unfazed, laughing as he told me about it. He responded to Paul that in fact, it was a "Daddy and Mommy" kind of arrangement—and then shocked Paul by saying, "And she's Daddy." He was right. I was the disciplinarian, the general on the field, the person who managed issues and decided what got escalated to Peter. In the article, Paul made the point "for most Liberal staffers, the most stressful call they can imagine will come from Sorbara." Peter wasn't bothered by Paul's question. My strength did not diminish him in any way, and gender was not a factor.

Lesson: Politics is like a family. The intensity of the work bonds you together as more than just colleagues. You stand together in good times and tough times.

Our time in Ottawa produced one of the most difficult personal moments I can recall. I will never forget being told the police were on the line and wanted to speak with someone in charge. My heart was pounding as I took the call, as we were already fretting that Mario Laguë had missed the morning staff meeting. Mario was a Canadian diplomat convinced by Peter to leave a senior job in Geneva to join us as the director of communications. The police informed me he had been killed on his way to work when his motorcycle collided with a truck that had turned illegally in front of him.

It was devastating, personally and professionally. We rallied around his family through the difficult days that followed. To honour Mario, we put together the best send-off we could, including former Prime Minister Paul Martin giving remarks at his memorial service, and a special celebration on the Hill, where his family was presented with the flag that flew over the Peace Tower on the day of his death.

Lesson: Choose being an accomplished professional over being popular.

My experience has shaped the advice I give to those fairly new to politics, particularly young people. If you want to be known as accomplished and professional, mediocrity is not an option. You do the best you can with every task you are handed. You pick people because they are the best for your team, and not just because they're your friends. You don't take shortcuts and settle for a less-than-exceptional presentation because it means missing a night out with friends. You don't go into meetings not having read the briefing notes. You don't scroll through your phone when you want to make an impression in the room. You act with integrity and strength of character.

I pressed staff hard to perform. When you are responsible for ensuring outcomes, you have no choice but to make sure the parts of the whole are operating efficiently and working in tandem. Some people responded well and performed beyond even their own expectations. Others were intimidated and struggled but kept going. And others failed utterly.

While working as chief operating officer for the leader of the opposition, two by-elections were called for November 29, 2010. It felt like two different realities: we were struggling to show momentum and we needed to be seen to be competitive against Harper's Conservatives. It was an opportunity for staff to show their mettle.

One was in Vaughan, caused by the resignation of long-time Liberal MP Maurizio Bevilacqua. We'd decided to fight hard for Vaughan as it had been a Liberal riding for twenty-two years. We were unable to recruit a strong candidate as no one as willing to run against Harper's star nominee, former Ontario Provincial Police commissioner Julian Fantino. We settled for long-time party organizer Tony Genco, leaving us at a distinct disadvantage. But I knew we could out-organize the Conservatives and prayed that at least some of the deep-rooted Liberal vote might hold.

The other by-election was in Winnipeg North, where veteran NDP member Judy Wasylycia-Leis had resigned to run for mayor of Winnipeg. It was assumed to be the tougher riding as it had been an NDP stronghold for over a decade. The Liberal hopes lay in star candidate Kevin Lamoureux, a popular Manitoba Liberal member of the legislative assembly who willingly made the leap to federal politics. If we had any chance of winning in that riding, we needed a warrior and there was no question Kevin was a warrior. We were only able to assign a small team from the Centre to fight for Winnipeg North as we could not afford the cost of travel and living arrangements. Kevin had a sizeable, dedicated group of local volunteers who would form the army, so I felt comfortable that what was needed most from the Centre were the generals to provide overall direction.

I drove both teams hard, but the Winnipeg team was essentially on its own. There was naturally some resentment as resources continued to pour into Vaughan, given its proximity to Toronto and that it was where I'd decided to focus. The team in Winnipeg, led by Matt Stickney, Zita Astravas, Azam Ishmael and Dave Ritchie, began to refer to themselves as the "B team" suggesting they were being treated as second-class citizens. That wasn't my intent, but I acknowledged that they felt that way. Still, they had a job to do and my response was, "If you act like the B team, then you'll always be the B team."

In the end, it was the B team who triumphed. We lost Vaughan by 997 votes but won Winnipeg North by 795 votes. Late on election night I was standing outside an RV belonging to Mark Roy, a Liberal senate staffer who had come from Ottawa to volunteer. I was drinking a beer and crank-calling Maurizio Bevilaqua (Maurizio had failed to help in any way and given the close margin, his endorsement could have made the difference) when my phone rang. It was the B team enjoying their well-earned moment of victory. They had won a close campaign and earned the right to crow about it.

Mediocrity does not win elections. Organization and discipline are non-negotiable. As my reputation for being tough and demanding had taken root, I thought of women who faced similar challenges: provincial Liberal Laura Miller, the NDP's Anne McGrath and Conservative Jenni Byrne to name a few. When we won, we were heroes, and everyone loved us. When we lost, we were demanding bitches who ran roughshod over people.

CHAPTER 5

Know Why You're in Politics
(or Take the Time to Figure It Out)

"Champions take responsibility. When the ball comes over the net, you can be sure I want the ball."
– Billie Jean King

After I returned from Ottawa in the summer of 2011, I was asked by Greg Sorbara to help Laura Albanese in the upcoming fall election in the provincial riding of York South-Weston. After losing the riding in the 2007 by-election by 315 votes, I had helped her win it back in the general election later that same year, by 452 votes. Greg can be very persuasive, and I agreed to oversee the 2011 campaign. Ultimately we held on once again, this time by 734 votes.

In the middle of the campaign Greg remarked that I should return to Queen's Park. Having no other plans post-election, I decided to check it out and made a few calls. One of those calls was to cabinet minister Kathleen Wynne. We had tea in her home and talked about the role of chief of staff in her office. We agreed it would be wonderful to collaborate, and talked about her leadership ambitions. We took the idea to Deb Roberts, who headed up human resources in the Office of the Premier. Deb agreed to take it forward.

The view quickly came back that the Centre felt it was not a good match. In the end, despite numerous overtures by both me and by Kathleen, working together was pronounced a no-go. Officially the reason was that I was an experienced chief who should be paired with a less-experienced minister. Put another way, Kathleen Wynne was a strong, veteran minister who did not need Pat Sorbara to steer the ship. But there was no doubt in my mind that it was leadership politics that stopped the coming together of a strong leadership contender with one of the most senior organizers in the party.

The low point of those discussions was when Kathleen called me and suggested I apply pressure by refusing any job with the government unless it was chief to her. I wanted to return to work and I was not about to threaten my friends. I also did not believe it would work with Deb Roberts (it would not have worked with me, if I were in Deb's role). I told Kathleen it was just not my style to give ultimatums. Whatever the reason, the Centre had made a decision and we needed to abide by it. It was a few days later that I was offered the role of chief of staff to the minister of education. I had never met the minister, Laurel Broten, but I was keen to make it work, and we did.

Lesson: Sometimes you have to consider the greater good and let the Centre do its job. But other times, the Centre ignores the front line at its peril.

The one thing political staff, civil servants and the party have in common is a relationship with the Centre, be it good or bad. The relationship with the Centre is likely to have the greatest impact on political staff. Learning to interact successfully with it can dictate the level of success ultimately achieved and, frankly, a person's enjoyment of their role. It makes a significant difference to the success of an elected official when their staff can work with the Centre to advance their agenda while understanding that from to time, the battle won't go their way. Senior staff in a minister's office act to bridge the Centre, the minister and the civil service.

Many come to feel the Centre is just a necessary evil, but it doesn't have to be that way. Working well, the Centre will drive the agenda and ensure the success of the individual elements of the overall organization. New governments tend to start by giving ministers as much autonomy as possible. Premiers and prime ministers go out of their way to say how much they believe in the ability of their ministers to do their jobs. And in most cases, they do. But in today's environment, where the overall brand is constantly under the microscope and tied so closely to the way the electorate views the leader, direction is needed in terms of what works and what detracts from the key messages of the government (or the goals of the opposition looking to replace them).

The best analogy I've found for a Centre working the way it should is air traffic control. You don't need to be flying every plane, and direct responsibility for the passengers on the planes lies with the pilots and the crew. But you sure as hell need to know where each plane is supposed to be going and how it intends to get there. You need to be immediately informed if a plane goes off course or is no longer on the radar.

From your position, you oversee all activity and ensure there are no mid-air collisions, that you are running the smoothest operation and that you can achieve the highest possible customer service satisfaction. Occasionally that means you may have to delay a plane, change a schedule or cancel a flight. Sometimes it means bringing a plane back to ground because of an unruly passenger. When you are in charge of air traffic control, you are constantly on alert for issues. You jump into action to manage an unexpected situation or avoid a crisis.

Good, smart leadership can come from the Centre, striving to balance the needs of all involved in the outcome of a decision. My early experience with the Centre shaped my outlook of it as a force for good. It helped me understand how decisions are made and how to make the relationship work, which was particularly helpful when I eventually left the cocoon and took on more responsibility as a chief of staff to a minister.

But not all leadership is excellent. In my experience, too often the Centre can become corrupted by the need for power and control, and by the fear of failure. The views of the outside world, mostly through media and polling, often have more sway over a decision than they should. The tougher things become, the more the Centre tends to withdraw unto itself, but I believe this is the exact time to reach out further. Over time, staffers tend to identify the Centre the way they would an individual or a whole organization, operating with a single mind or point of view.

I always bristle when told, "I've talked to the Centre, and this is what they want us to do," or "I got a call from the Premier's Office." These are overwrought phrases that suggest the people at the Centre work as a monolith. They do not. I always asked, "Who did you talk to?" And based on the answer, I'd assess next steps. Sometimes I'd go with it, sometimes I'd verify and sometimes I'd push back. That's not easy for everyone to do, as the notion of the Centre is scary for most people in politics.

Trust is endowed by the Centre when it has confidence around how an issue will be managed, that it will be brought forward in a timely fashion and that the Centre will never be caught off guard by a development. Hundreds of hours are spent reviewing media (including social media) and talking with stakeholders in order to manage what is being said about an issue. By carefully coordinating the Centre, the Minister's office and the civil service, good news (new programs or legislation) and bad news (an ice storm, school strike) can be managed equally well.

If the situation is not under control, the Centre is obligated to move into crisis management. If the circumstances reach a high level of tension, the Ministry and civil servants can be left behind as the Centre moves quickly to bring the situation back into manageable parameters. If you are not glued to your email at that point in time, the decision will be made to move forward without you. At the make-or-break point, staffers and elected officials will shine or be left in the dust.

Under the best circumstances, the Centre will consult everyone involved in deciding how to manage an issue, including external stakeholders. But circumstances are rarely ideal. It requires discipline and commitment to follow protocol and not take the easiest route available to you. I spent much of my time in politics working to create and implement protocols for moments of crisis. It was tough. The tendency is to panic and make quick decisions without awaiting the needed input or direction. Often folks hope to cover a mistake before it is widely known so they involve as few people as possible, or they bypass others on the organization chart and get a decision from the most senior person around. That's particularly true when the direction given by the Centre was ignored or it backfired. My advice to staffers is to inform the Centre as soon as a problem is identified. My holding line has long been, "It's far better to let us help you solve a problem when it's still a problem and before it becomes a full-fledged crisis."

Whether it's working well or struggling significantly, I believe in the Centre. To go back to my air traffic control analogy, without the Centre politics would truly be left to the chaos and repercussions of hundreds of mid-air collisions. There must be hierarchy, direction and discipline. The question is when it acts as an iron fist and when it is a firm, guiding hand. I have spent a lot of time at the Centre and a lot of time thinking about it. In my experience, it can play a very healthy role in a political organization, or it can be the reason that a party fails in its effort to win the next election.

Problems happen when the Centre decides it knows better than everyone else. Ideally, each part of the overall organization does its work and makes recommendations to the Centre. Instead of two-way communication between equals, the Centre will give direction (often without a real understanding of the issue) and the groups impacted are expected to implement it without question or complaint. The short-term result is a bad decision being implemented for the wrong reasons. The longer-term outcome is a significant level of bitterness that brings about bad decisions, information being withheld, waning support (and sometimes outright vitriol) for the Centre, and a serious disconnect with the ground troops.

While most of my time in politics has been at the Centre, I've always tried to stay in touch with those within the larger organization.

People would ask me why I took time away from my role in the Premier's Office to work full-time on a by-election. Of course part of it was my love of by-elections. More importantly was the opportunity to see how the ground was working and to hear directly from voters. It connected me to party staff and volunteers. It was a way to demonstrate that I cared about who was up and coming in the party, and who got things done (and to learn their names).

That's not to say I haven't played the role of the bad guy from the Centre. I have done this so many times and I have the nasty emails (and in the old days, faxes) to prove it. At the same time, I worked to stay true to my roots by taking time to explain the rationale and debate a decision. Ensuring someone was consulted or felt part of the discussion helped relationships survive a decision by the Centre. Much of it was having the guts to tell the truth about why a decision was made, rather than making up excuses no one believed. I tried to ensure the voice of the ground was heard at the Centre.

In a by-election, I took time to ask staff what they were hearing at the door and how they felt things were going. That led to some funny moments, as many people new to Liberal politics were aware of my name but did not always recognize me in person. Occasionally in a campaign office, I would be standing amongst a group of canvassers, getting their feedback. A person would hold out their hand and say, "Hi, I'm Jack." I'd shake their hand and say, "Hi, I'm Pat Sorbara." The reaction would be priceless, particularly if it was a staff person who had just finished providing an opinion constructively critical of the campaign or the Centre. I'd laugh and assure them they were not in any trouble, that I welcomed their feedback.

Lesson: Civil servants can be your best friend or your worst enemy. The goal is always to make them your best friend.

Civil servants work with government to find the best way to meet the goals articulated during an election or through a policy announcement. Realizing the government is likely to find a way regardless, the civil servant is best positioned, and in my mind obligated, to help to find the most effective, least negative way of delivering on the commitment. The civil servant tends to know the stakeholders best. Nothing hurts a government more than an announcement getting immediately panned by the people it's designed to help.

Civil servants are very powerful in shaping an issue or outcome because they control the information and are set up to do the work and research better than the much smaller group of political staff who buffer the elected government and have many other priorities. You can demand the civil service create a report, but you can't tell them what must be in it.

In my experience there is always room for a civil servant to express a point of view and engage in the debate. It's helpful and it's healthy and it doesn't make them partisan. The only caveat is that at the end of day they accept that it's the politician who gets to give the direction and make the decision. In other words, they are there to advise and support the goals of the government, but they are not political.

Too often political staff believe that the civil service works for the politician when in fact the civil service must act without bias toward the party in power. Having said that, civil servants have diverse backgrounds and will naturally have a personal political leaning. In my experience, understanding politics is an asset for a civil servant, but they must be disciplined enough not to inject it into their advice. Ideally the political operation and the civil service work closely on the outcomes critical to the government. When each are doing their jobs, and maintain a level of mutual respect, it works exceptionally well.

My best experience of how the civil service supports a government initiative was in 2012. When the Centre invited me to become chief of staff to Minister Broten, they asked me about one specific issue: 2012 would be the year we'd undertake negotiations with the entire education sector and it wasn't expected to be an easy road. Did I think I could handle it? I said yes but I had no idea what I had gotten myself into.

"Not an easy road" was an understatement. After several years of building up the education system, with millions of dollars in new investments, it was time to reduce spending. We were given a savings target and ministry officials developed several approaches that would get us there, none of them expected to be acceptable to the unions and in most cases, the school boards either. Tempers flared early and it took many meetings over several months before we were able to come anywhere near a set of terms and conditions acceptable to anyone.

It was when we were getting closer to a deal with the Ontario English Catholic Teachers' Association (OECTA) that I witnessed the civil service truly working their magic. Under the direction of a senior negotiator and labour relations lawyer named Paul Boniferro (who later became Ontario's deputy attorney general), ministry officials Gabriel Sekaly and Andrew Davis somehow found a way to create the conditions for what we hoped would finalize a deal with OECTA and form the foundation for the rest of the system. We were holed up together in the Sheraton Centre in downtown Toronto, working long days, weekends and even a few all-nighters. They ran the numbers and calculated scenarios, wrote proposals and answered questions while somehow doing their day jobs. It was something to behold.

The process did not end well, to say the least. Regardless, the experience was like nothing I'd ever witnessed before. It was incredible to watch senior lawyers, civil servants, political staff and the minister pull together as a team to do what was essentially the impossible. Everyone stayed in their lanes and did their jobs but the team environment was upbeat and positive. For me, it had the feeling of a campaign. We pulled together in the tough moments, helped each other through the fatigue and kept focused on the needed outcome.

However, it's not unusual for politicians, or political staff acting on their behalf, to clash with the recommendations put forward by the civil service. Generally it's around what's possible under the law, the timeline and the commitment of dollars to projects. Political staff will push the envelope to reach a particular outcome. Civil servants will tend to try to maintain the status quo and ensure the politician understands the implications of the decision, particularly if it represents a significant change to the way things have been done in the past.

The toughest circumstances tend to arise when elected officials are under pressure to deliver specific projects for their ridings. In some cases, the commitment was made during their campaigns, having no idea what it would take to deliver on it. Among the most common examples is a new school or money for renovations so a school can stay open. The capital budget in the Ministry of Education is based on a complicated formula and on input from school boards. At the end of that process, recommendations for the assignment of capital comes to the political level. Civil servants tend to expect, and hope for, a quick sign-off on the recommendations as presented. In the meantime, the minister will have been extensively lobbied by MPPs from all parties, pressured by their communities to deliver schools for their particular areas.

Political staff are obligated to dig deep enough to see if the political demand has merit, based on information from the elected official. Political staff will overlay elements that may have been overlooked, or that are higher priorities for the elected government. There may be more to the story than what local officials have told the ministry. It may be that the priorities of the civil service are not aligned with those of the minister. In the final round, the political round, changes can still be made, but the reasons for the change have to be defended.

To the outside world, politics is always about politicians. Very little is known about the people who work every day behind the scenes as government employees. Even fewer can differentiate between a non-partisan, non-political civil servant who serves the government, and the political staff person attached directly to a politician who walks the line between the beliefs and priorities of the party in power, and the government for which they work. Government consulting agencies often make considerable money teaching clients how to understand the difference in the roles, as well as educating them on how decisions are made.

The differentiation is critical and should not be as mysterious as it appears to be. Political staff serve as the check-and-balance point between what the government wants to get done and what the civil service says is doable. It's here where political staff do their real work and are often the unsung heroes of an outcome. They are the ones who think, research, consult and dialogue in the search for a solution to a difficult problem. They are masterful at thinking outside the box and pushing the civil service outside of its comfort zone. They talk the language of stakeholders and are often best positioned to use reason and reality to push a workable compromise. With good faith and the right people at the table, both internal and external, most issues can get to resolution. And if they can't, the reasons are documented and understood. Then the communications staff take over to build up the good news and manage the bad.

At the end of the day, civil servants can stand between success or failure on a file. You must treat a member of the civil service with respect and acknowledge that their role is different from yours. Listen to their advice and fully consider their views and experience. They will know more about the file than any political staff will ever know. Keep the civil service up to date on the decisions being made, even if those decisions are different from the ones they recommend. Working in sync, much can be achieved in a very short time, with fewer forced errors.

Lesson: No matter how accomplished you are, when you punch above your weight, you're going to feel like a fraud. Keep the faith and keep going.

The toughest lesson for me, which haunted me throughout my career, was overcoming the deep-seated fear that someone would figure out I was a fraud. In many environments in which I ultimately excelled, I had to fight the voice in my head that constantly told me I had no business being there, that people could see right through me. Whether it was as the CEO of a growing software company or in a senior government or campaign role, I would convince myself I was going to fail. It kept me up at night and it was my motivation, driving me forward. The trick was to balance the fear with a "fuck you, nothing will stop me" attitude.

I knew much of that had to do with being a woman. Over the years the most frequent message I heard was, "A woman doesn't belong here." The energy sector, which I first experienced as chief of staff to the minister of energy in 1987 but encountered again in the private sector at Superior Propane and Advanced, was not welcoming to women. In general, the sector was downright resistant. That meant there were few role models or places to turn for advice. And sadly, sometimes successful women in the field were reluctant to admit there was even a problem, despite the evidence being all around us.

When I started at Advanced, one of the earliest hurdles was negotiating contracts with clients. It was complex, steeped in legalese and it could take months. From time to time, I'd be at a meeting with potential shareholders or bank officials, often as the only woman in the room. I remember once, when we were looking for an investor for the company, we were in a boardroom waiting for the start of the meeting when I started to shake. I remember tears threatening as I said, "I can't do this. I have no business being here. They are going to know I am a fraud." We delayed the start for a few minutes as my business partners and our lawyer Jay Feldman assured me they had my back. With their support, I pulled myself together the way I had done so many times in politics. There was no choice but to forge ahead—both in the meeting and as a company.

In the end I had to trust my gut. There was no way to sustain the pressure and simultaneously do excellent work. These moments of imposter syndrome have resurfaced from time to time over the years: when I returned to Queen's Park as chief of staff to Laurel Broten years later, I was thrilled to be given a role at the Ministry of Education. Given the amount of experience I had to that point, I welcomed the challenge of working in an area I knew little about, with the added bonus of going into labour negotiations with the entire education sector. It was a massive undertaking and I had no idea what would be involved.

I recall the first day sitting with government lawyers, civil servants and outside labour consultants, and wondering what the hell I was doing there. Yes, I represented the minister, but I felt I had little to offer in terms of the details or the approach to negotiating. It became even more intense when one of the union negotiators zoned in on me, saying I was the only person with whom they were prepared to engage, given that the decisions to be made would rise to the political level.

Despite my fear, I leaned on my instincts. I spent time getting to know which civil servants at the table I could trust. I reached out to the only other person in the room who had once been a political staffer, albeit a Conservative one. Paul Boniferro led the team of outside labour consultants; he needed me to interact with the politicians and I needed him to help me understand the game plan each day. It reached the point where he and I together briefed the minister and the Centre. I still said very little at the table but at the end of the day, only Paul and the senior ministry officials who took me under their wings knew that on most days, I was flying by the seat of my pants.

It was an incredibly tense number of months, but I got to the other side thanks to working hard, keeping everyone involved and informed and leaning on others to help me through. Being centrally involved in that messy and thrilling yet scary period of time gave me an experience like no other I've ever had, and I gained a few friends.

Lesson: In politics, everything is urgent. "Urgent" means different things to different people, and you have to learn how to manage priorities.

Political staff directly control the world in which the politician lives. For a minister, premier or prime minister, that means deciding daily—sometimes hourly—which issue or event is given priority. "It's urgent" is a common phrase around government. It's up to political staff to decide if an issue requires immediate access to the politician or whether it could wait a few hours, days or even a few weeks. And sometimes the decision is that the issue does not require the attention of the politician at all, and it is sent to a staffer or a civil servant for resolution.

Some political staff think it's best to limit civil service access to the minister. It's always been my view that if a deputy minister wants to see the minister, access should be granted. Maybe not always on the timetable requested but certainly the access needs to be arranged. The deputy minister is the person who ultimately pushes through the agenda on the civil service side and when there is a good working relationship, issues are resolved quickly and successfully. The question for me was whether that meeting should be one on one, or if the chief of staff to the minister should be in the room. The answer depended on two things: the minister's decision-making process and the relationship between the chief and the deputy.

A minister with experience will know how to handle a direct request from a deputy, and particularly when to involve political staff or the Centre before responding. That's a critical line and mistakes are made when an inexperienced minister concedes to the wishes of the deputy without consulting the political side of the office. Ministers are human beings and as politicians, generally want to be liked. As a result, for a less experienced minister it's safer to have their chief in the room during meetings with the deputy.

In most cases, the working relationship between the deputy and the political staff is positive and professional. But not always. On occasion the deputy's own ambition gets in the way of the government's political agenda, or the demands of the minister's office are deemed unreasonable. Compromise can be reached by balancing the need for the government to accomplish its agenda with the realities presented by the data and experience of the bureaucrats. If the relationship works well, the political staff can push the civil service beyond the status quo. Equally, the civil service can ensure that the political agenda will not falter because it was rushed.

In my entire time in the public service, there were very few moments I felt at odds with a deputy minister, but it happened occasionally. It was normal to debate priorities or sort out a staffing issue. The only time I clashed directly was when a deputy went to the Centre directly without my knowledge. And in the case of the 2012–13 education negotiations, the deputy provided updates to the Centre that conflicted directly with the information I was providing, and eventually I had to call him on it. It was costing too much time and energy to do damage control.

Deputies report to the secretary of cabinet and that is where concerns are to be raised. The secretary to cabinet is positioned to bring the issue to the Centre, if deemed necessary. Deputies who try to work around their ministers and political staff generally do so in a direct attempt to change the outcome of a decision made by the minister, or because they seek to build their personal profiles with the Centre. It shouldn't happen because it results in confusion and blurs the lines of the role of the civil service.

Lesson: Political staff have to be prepared to speak truth to power.

The job of political staff is to advise elected officials on the issues. Many believe that means saying yes to the politician, no matter the consequences, or finding a way to realize their agenda no matter the cost. Newsflash: it doesn't.

A staffer needs to ensure a minister understands the full picture. That means discussing all the elements of an issue even if the minister isn't interested in the debate. If you're lucky, everything aligns and the decision is straightforward. But more often, the decision is layered. Staff provide their best advice, check with the Centre when necessary and ensure a decision can be defended. It is only then the politician can make a well-informed decision.

If you are in opposition, the primary consideration is politics and your goal is to be elected and replace the government. The same obligation exists to consider all elements before taking a position on an issue, but often the only critical factor is what will hurt the government most. That's not the way it should be; public discourse has been seriously harmed by the hyper-partisan world in which we all now live. It has become the role of the opposition to oppose for opposition's sake only. There is rarely an attempt to achieve good government by working together when warranted. This is perhaps the saddest reality of today's political world.

CHAPTER 6

You Win as a Team, You Lose as a Team

> "It's not for the ring, it's not for the championship. It's for the
> testimony that if people come together they can become part of
> something bigger than themselves. And it's a real story."
> – VENUS WILLIAMS

After the leadership race in which Kathleen Wynne took over as premier, she demoted Laurel Broten to the role of minister of intergovernmental affairs. It was confirmed for me by many that Laurel was almost left completely out of cabinet. Premier Wynne was unhappy with the way negotiations had proceeded with the education sector. The McGuinty team had decided to play hardball, and they were prepared to push the unions to the brink. It was ugly and negative and—in the long term—unhealthy to the relationship between the government and key education stakeholders.

Kathleen had been minister of education at the time that Premier McGuinty revelled in his role as "the education premier." She had led the way out of the wilderness brought about by the Harris government and nursed the education system back to a viable entity where teachers felt valued and students were positioned to succeed. Of course, that meant lots of money was flowing into the system and major issues, including class sizes, were being addressed. It also meant that teachers and unions felt they were in the driver's seat with this government. And despite how much they had gained since the

Liberals formed government in 2003, the unions were not remotely prepared to balance the ledger even a little in 2012.

In the midst of the negotiations with the education sector, Premier McGuinty made all leadership candidates resign from cabinet. No longer a cabinet minister, Kathleen Wynne felt much freer to criticize the efforts of the government, led by Minister Broten, to reach a negotiated settlement with the education unions. Although she did not come out publicly on it, she was backchannelling her views to her contacts inside and outside of government, as well as to the sector itself. I could hear the voice of Kathleen Wynne at the cabinet table even after she'd left, as her views were being represented by her supporters still in cabinet.

I felt caught in the middle of two strong, brilliant women. They were equally committed to their very different views on how to proceed. Kathleen needed the unions to support her in the leadership race, so politically, she did not want them to walk away from the Liberal Party before the next election. Laurel was focused on delivering the short-term marching orders we had been given by the Premier's Office. As we were in the midst of this difficult process, Laurel also had to accept that these extremely fraught and controversial negotiations had spoiled any chance she may have had to run for leader. By then, the political environment around her was just too poisoned.

Although I had understood them to be friends, Kathleen and Laurel rarely spoke directly to one another during this period, which only served to increase the distance between them. As I continued to do my job as chief of staff to Minister Broten, including representing her on the negotiating team, Kathleen had just stopped speaking to me. It was clear she considered me part of the problem.

Lesson: There are so many twists and turns in politics that you never know what awaits around the next corner. Or who. If you are in politics for the right reason, it's important to be open to changing circumstances.

After she was elected leader of the Ontario Liberal Party, Kathleen sat down with every single member of caucus. I remember being very impressed by that decision—it was smart in that she was looking to unite the team behind her but at the same time, it showed tremendous respect to her caucus colleagues, even those who had not supported her.

Laurel left her meeting with Kathleen feeling it had gone well and that they had cleared the air. Kathleen had asked Laurel why she chose to support leadership candidate Sandra Pupatello over her, and Laurel answered honestly that she felt Sandra was the better person to lead the province at a time of economic challenge. It was clear Kathleen had been hurt by Laurel's decision not to support her but leaving that meeting, Laurel still believed she was in line for a senior economic portfolio.

A few nights later, I received a call from a devastated Laurel. Kathleen had made her minister of intergovernmental affairs, a portfolio with no real role attached to it because the premier always represents the government at intergovernmental situations. The message of distrust and punishment was clear.

I was shocked that Premier Wynne had demoted one of the smartest, most capable women I had ever met in politics. She put her need to demonstrate to the unions that she had punished those responsible for the last round of negotiations ahead of finding a way to keep a strong, successful woman in politics. The decision set the path for Laurel to resign her seat, leave politics and move to the east coast in support of her husband's career. In January 2015, she was appointed president and CEO of Nova Scotia Business Inc. Nova Scotia's gain was, without a doubt, Ontario's loss.

The change also meant I would be out of a job as soon as Laurel departed. Given that the new premier had made it clear she was unhappy with me too, I packed up my boxes, helped our staff find jobs in other ministries and was preparing to leave government (again—this would be the third time I'd done this in my career). I had a meeting scheduled on Tuesday with Tom Teahen, the chief of staff to Premier Wynne, to negotiate my exit.

In a strange twist, though, the previous Friday I began to get urgent calls from Melissa Branco, the assistant to my friend David Herle, insisting I join David for lunch on Monday. I hadn't talked with David in a while, so I assumed something was up. I explained that I was expecting to have lots of time in the near future and could plan a visit, but Melissa insisted it had to be Monday and didn't know why it was all so urgent.

Somewhat begrudgingly, I said fine and showed up at noon on Monday to a restaurant called Gusto on King Street West in Toronto, and proceeded to have one of the most fateful discussions of my life. At that lunch David confided in me that the premier had asked him to take on the role of campaign chair for the upcoming election. We were in a minority government and the election could be triggered at any time. Kathleen felt her campaign organization needed an overhaul. David told me his response to the premier was that he was prepared to take the role on one condition: that Pat Sorbara join the campaign as the campaign manager who would run the day-to-day.

David has good and honest friends who've long helped him understand that organization is not his strength. He is a strategic thinker and communicator—one of the best in the country. But a political campaign requires an air war and a ground war. Done right, the two will work in tandem and weave a masterful approach to a winning campaign strategy. So, to do his best work at the air war level, David knew he needed a ground war general to match his efforts. On the recommendation of one of the co-chairs, Tim Murphy, and a few others, he decided I was that person.

The phrase "I nearly fell off my chair" fits well here. I withdrew into myself for about twenty seconds, holding onto the bottom of my chair (so I wouldn't actually fall off it). I was sure Kathleen Wynne and the leadership team around her were truly done with me. And once I'd recovered enough to talk, I asked David those questions. He said that the premier had suggested something similar, and that she was not at all sure I'd be willing to stay and take a leadership role in her campaign.

David was probably one of the only people who could have con-vinced me to stay. I was not sure I wanted to work for a party with Kathleen Wynne at the helm, given how she had acted to undermine the education-sector negotiations and how she had treated Laurel Broten. But I believed in the Ontario Liberal Party and by extension in Kathleen Wynne enough to give it my full consideration.

There was a combination of things that brought me to a yes, in addition to the opportunity to work with David again (we'd known each other from the 1990 Paul Martin leadership campaign, where our friendship first developed) but my signing on didn't come with-out conditions.

Top of the list was the title of the very senior role I was being of-fered. David called it campaign manager, but I told him I would need the title "campaign director." He asked me why it mattered. I gave him the first of a number of lectures on why titles help to crystallize who is in charge and that for a woman, it is a necessary signal of leadership to the rest of the team. I said I would not take "manager" as that was the title used at the local riding level. As well, Don Guy (a friend I have known since the Lyn McLeod days and the person who had run the campaigns for Dalton McGuinty) had always held the title of campaign director. If there was a sign that I was truly in charge of the day-to-day of the campaign, that would be it.

Next up, I said I needed to have the room to do the job. To real-ly do the job. This meant I was not going to be overruled without consultation. It was not the first time I had been asked to take the second-in-command role. I was happy to take this position (it's where I believe I do my best work) but I wanted to be sure the role was real.

My last caveat was that I would need to talk with the premier. I wouldn't take the role unless I was sure she truly wanted me to have it. We would be working closely together and, given the frosty encounters we'd had in recent months, I needed to be sure that she wanted me on the team and hadn't been talked into the decision.

It took a few weeks before I saw the premier and by the time the meeting was arranged, I had pretty much agreed I would take the role. Truthfully, I was thrilled. The role was daunting in that it seemed the organization was not that far along, and we were living in an uncertain world based on the minority situation. It is always difficult to integrate into an existing team and the premier had staffed the Centre with many of the same people who ran or were involved in her leadership bid. I was not at all sure what I was walking into, but I definitely knew I wanted to go down that road to figure it out.

When I finally sat down with Premier Wynne, our conversation covered the remaining ground I needed to address. The premier admitted she was not at all sure I would take the role for the same reasons I felt she would not want me on her team. We reminded each other of the earlier attempt to work with one another, when we were thwarted by the then Premier's Office.

We agreed that going forward, she and I would never discuss the education file because our differences of opinion were simply too great to find common ground. That was fine with me, and I only broke from that agreement whenever I had to intervene to correct the facts of an issue being discussed at the senior staff table. We also discussed my reputation as a demanding manager. I looked Kathleen in the eye and stated, "You know I have earned a reputation as a tough boss. You need to understand it's because I am one. I demand the best of everyone, and I do the job to the fullest. That means you'll get complaints about me, but you'll also always be sure the job will get done." She acknowledged her awareness of my reputation and said she needed my organizational skills, determination and discipline. Together, we agreed I would take the role of campaign director.

I cannot tell you the excitement and joy I felt in that moment. My years of hard work and experience had finally propelled me to the peak of my career and the bonus would be that if successful, Kathleen Wynne would be the first woman to be elected premier of Ontario.

Lesson: Work harder than everyone else and don't settle for less than your best.

Anyone who wanted to work with me had to accept the reality that I was tough on people and pushed them to do better, be more creative, problem-solve, work harder and never settle for second-rate. In campaigns, that meant strictly adhering to the approved canvass strategy, achieving the ID target and updating daily the charts on the wall that measured progress. It meant complete discipline around the candidate. And if you had a key role, you attended the morning and evening meetings every day, prepared to give an update. For party events and larger projects, though, it was more challenging to ensure outcomes.

When I began my work as Ontario Liberal Party campaign director in late 2013, I joined a team that was disjointed and operating in a bubble. Most had been involved in the unexpected, come-from-behind victory by Kathleen Wynne at the leadership convention and gone directly into roles in the Premier's Office. The first challenge was to make sure they understood the true nature of their roles, both in government and what they would do in a campaign, and to focus them on the long game: the upcoming election.

The party's annual general meeting (AGM) was held in March 2014 and would be the last before the general election. I wanted to maximize every moment of the three-day event, with an agenda that included training sessions on campaign activity to candidate photos and media training, to events to showcase the leader and team. After considerable discussion, the campaign leadership decided to use the AGM to launch the pre-writ campaign, highlighting our strategy to be ready for the general election that could be called as early as May.

The party was happy to work with the campaign team to turn the AGM into a campaign event. Staff involved in panel sessions seemed shocked when I asked to see their presentations well in advance so I could review them and give comments. They needed to be entertaining and informative. I changed up panels to add subject matter experts and volunteers. I scheduled a rehearsal for every panel so I could provide feedback and deal with redundant messaging.

There was a lot of grumbling about forcing people who had done presentations for years to prepare and rehearse. But for me the only thing that mattered was providing the delegates, who would be paying a lot of money to be there, our best effort in the form of a professional program. In doing so, we would look ready and focused on the campaign. It wasn't personal, it was business. And we needed to deliver value to the attendees.

Nominated candidates were the next priority. It was important they developed a sense of team and an understanding of their roles. All staff were required to show up Friday morning to attend a session outlining the goals of the AGM and what we needed from them (the added advantage was that it forced them to be on-site to attend Friday afternoon training sessions). During my presentation to staff, I put up a photo of every nominated candidate and asked them to seek them out and introduce themselves. Candidates were on the front line and the more they knew the team supporting them, the better.

I was able to convince the co-chairs to have a large rally and open it to people from the downtown Toronto ridings. To demonstrate momentum, we'd need one thousand people. I was constantly reminded that it was a high-risk strategy. What if no one showed up? What if the media thought it was silly to have a rally so early in the pre-writ? What if it was a flat event?

High-risk was my speciality. More so, my reaction to being told something could not be done was to prove people wrong. I knew that by reviewing the details over and over, the risk factor would be seriously reduced. It meant the appearance of the room had to be high-tech and high-end. It meant knowing exactly who was responsible to deliver people to the rally, and triple-checking that each riding had a plan to meet its commitment. It meant walking through the details of the program many times to ensure it ran without a hitch and having a dress rehearsal on the stage. It meant a high performance by the premier as she launched her team of candidates and her campaign.

The AGM weekend was a remarkable success. The feedback was outstanding, and delegates left feeling good about our chances of re-election. The media referenced momentum and organizational strength. Most importantly, the large team of individuals who had worked incredibly hard in the lead-up and over the weekend knew they had delivered their best and were proud of their contributions to the campaign launch.

On a daily basis, I demanded the same level of performance as I did in campaigns and key party events. I required people be on time for meetings and if they were delayed, to send an email to let their supervisors know why. I expected them to take notes and follow up on their assignments. It was important to update the right people and share information. To be known as a high-performing political staffer, you had to work hard, meet deadlines and show results.

I held myself to the same standard I demanded of others. I rarely left a campaign headquarters ahead of the team. I stayed as late as I needed to ensure everything was ready for the next day. I'd rework a presentation over and over until I believed it was the best it could be. I conducted post-mortems and debriefs to determine how we could do better next time.

Lesson: Protocols and processes are essential to any organization that seeks to be successful. Politics is no exception.

The months between August 2013 and May 2014 were challenging on so many levels. I was far from welcomed by most of the existing staff around the premier at Queen's Park. The same was true for the existing campaign team, such as it was. They felt they were doing a great job and that change was not needed. Some of them circled the wagons around Tom Allison (who had managed the leadership campaign for Kathleen Wynne and who seemed to have claimed the role of campaign director) and tried to work around me. Anyone who has worked with me knows that it's simply not an option to work around me. Things got tense pretty fast.

The other immediate and significant issue was the assumption that everyone working in the Premier's Office would have a role in the campaign, and likely one similar to their government role (meaning, for example, that a communications advisor in the Premier's Office would be a communications advisor in the campaign). While it is often the case that roles and people overlap, the bigger concern is ensuring you have the best person in place for each job, and this wasn't always the case. On top of that, it has always been my belief that a campaign team needs to have a mix of individuals who work with the leader on a daily basis and people from outside of that core. It means that new ideas and new energy are injected into the process. Any existing, unhealthy working relationships can be managed by separating or adding to existing teams. A role would be found for everyone involved but it may not be the role the person wanted or assumed they would have.

Despite the tension and general resistance, I began to build the campaign structure and team. I produced an organization chart and chose someone to lead each of the major areas we needed to cover—everything from office management to tour direction. I reached out to people outside of Queen's Park, and I met with everyone (or at least everyone I could manage) who had expressed interest in working on the campaign. In most cases, I encouraged people to look for roles at the local level where the greatest number of resources would be needed. Everyone believes the central campaign is more important and exciting, but the riding level requirements are overlooked at a party's peril.

One of my major efforts was to ensure the work being done by government and the political work heading into an election were integrated. This was achieved through the creation of many systems, processes and protocols. There was considerable resistance to this structure and planning, but my general mantra was "resistance is futile." If you wanted to be part of the campaign, you needed to work within and respect the structure in place, and to accept there was a hierarchy to be followed.

I have found that generally people believe that structure and process are not possible in politics, because of its incredibly ad hoc nature. You can plan your day, but it takes only one event (major or minor) to throw it into chaos and upend the priorities (we're not talking catastrophe either—it could be as simple as an ice storm, a damaging report by an external organization, a cabinet minister shot-gunning on an issue, a delayed briefing because the minister is required elsewhere, and even a taped phone conversation with a potential candidate).

The reality is that in those moments of chaos and confusion, hierarchy, structure and discipline save the day. Staff know who to call in a crisis, who to update, who needs to be involved in the decisions, when to wait for further direction and when to just go. People who have experienced it know it can be tough to admit a mistake, or that trouble is brewing. The ability to understand the potential impact of an issue before it becomes a crisis is absolutely necessary to prevent further damage and bring the issue under control quickly. Those who have not experienced it, or did not act when needed, have failed to learn some of the more critical lessons politics has to offer.

At the senior level we found cohesion fairly quickly. Tom Teahen and Andrew Bevan, as the leaders in government, met with me and David Herle weekly. In those meetings we discussed issues and aired grievances or concerns. Priorities were set, solutions were found and we acted as the senior team.

We had a small group who met regularly with the leader to keep her up to date and get her input. I called it "the kitchen cabinet." Those gatherings included David Herle, Andrew Bevan, Tom Teahen, Jane Rounthwaite, Deb Matthews and Tim Murphy from time to time, and me. These meetings almost always happened in Kathleen and her partner Jane's living room. We had tea and homemade muffins and talked through the challenges—always with an eye to solutions. My job was to ensure we stayed on track and had a plan to execute the decisions made, which sometimes meant explaining why some ideas weren't workable. If there was difficult information to be shared with the leader, such as bad polling numbers, it happened at those gatherings.

Some of the toughest decisions were made in that living room. A few major personnel changes had to be made, including removing

Tom Allison from the equation. He had become very angry when I told him that he would not have a key role in the campaign, given his unwillingness to accept and support my appointment to campaign director. Tom's anger impacted my ability to move staff forward in terms of the way I wanted to run the campaign. It was unfortunate and given my long history of friendship with Tom, and my respect for his commitment to the party, I have always felt badly about it. But it represented an example of where the intended outcome came ahead of the person. I simply could not do my best work if there was even a whiff of confusion in terms of who was in charge.

Then there was the integration committee, comprised of a larger group of people who sorted through the many competing demands for the premier's time. It overlaid the priorities of the government, the caucus, the leader's constituency, the party and the campaign. I chaired that committee with Bob Lopinski in his role as head of the war room. One of Tom Teahen or Andrew Bevan was always in the room, along with David Herle. People came prepared to fight for time and justify priorities. It could be long and painful, but in the lead-up to the campaign, it ensured that the focus was on the areas of greatest importance as decided by the team who would run the campaign.

On the campaign side, I established an operations committee whose members included the directors of each major area of the campaign. There, the focus was solely on being ready to run a thirty-seven-day campaign no matter when it would take place. We debated the tour plans, the placement of resources, the budget requirements, opposition watch, fundraising and organization. Candidate search and local riding support were central to every discussion, as we kept the focus on targeted ridings considered winnable.

Lesson: The Girl Guide motto applies to politics—always be prepared. At least as prepared as you can be.

Hurtling toward a campaign in an unknown time frame (due to the minority government situation) meant it was always tense. No matter how much was accomplished each week, I always felt key things were not getting done, and we were constantly debating scenarios. I clearly remember the day David Herle turned to me and said, "What happens if Andrea Horwath refuses to support the budget and we find ourselves in an election overnight?" Did we have a headquarters? Did we have a launch plan? Was the bus ready to go? Although we were reasonably confident the NDP would want to avoid a campaign, knowing their level of readiness was poor, his question focused my priority list.

It was a fucking good thing it had. I remember very well sitting in the Liberal Caucus Service Bureau (LCSB) boardroom with a group of staff on the morning of May 2, 2014, watching an NDP press conference. While we were preparing for the very situation we were watching unfold, it was still a shock to hear Horwath say the NDP would not support the budget. We swung into action and began to ready ourselves to go immediately. I breathed a sigh of relief knowing that the buses were in storage nearby, and that the wraps would be dry by Monday. But I fretted that the campaign headquarters needed some work and that we still needed a few more candidates.

One major pressure point for any campaign is filling its slate of candidates. We still needed a handful. Barrie was the last seat filled and we were close to convincing a staff person to run there. At the last moment we were able to recruit a great candidate in Ann Hoggarth, an elementary school teacher and union leader who for some reason jumped into the fray at the last minute. (Despite that riding being a long shot, she won it.) On May 13, I was proud to tweet out that we were the first party to have nominated all 107 candidates.

It became clear the NDP felt they had a few weeks to get up and running, as they assumed the government would go through the legislative process of trying to pass the budget and they, together with Tim Hudak's Conservatives, would vote to bring down the government. Instead, that afternoon Premier Wynne visited Lieutenant-Governor David C. Onley and asked him to dissolve the 40th

Parliament of Ontario, clearing the way for an election to be called five days later, sending Ontario to the polls on June 12. The day may have started with the NDP having the upper hand, but it ended with the Liberals pulling the rug out from under them. It felt amazing.

From time to time, I was reminded of my place and it happened on that day. David left the room saying he'd been called to meet with Andrew, Tom and the premier to discuss next steps. It felt uncomfortable to be left out of such a discussion, but that is sometimes the fate of the second-in-command. I am sure it would have been fine if I had tagged along, but that was not my style—I was not so self-important as to believe I had to be in every meeting. It was when I felt intentionally excluded that I had an issue. No matter what they decided, we were having an election and we'd have to execute the strategy they'd settle on. It made more sense to stay put and begin to work on the plan we had put into place.

That same evening, May 2, we had a large kickoff event in downtown Toronto. It looked to the media that we had magically pulled together hundreds of people to take part. It was a coincidence that there was already a staff gathering planned for that evening, providing a base of at least three hundred people. By opening the invitation to downtown Toronto Liberals, we easily drew a large and enthusiastic crowd. We happily took the credit, but it came down to always being ready to take advantage of a winning hand.

I did not attend the party that evening (Are you kidding? We had a campaign starting the next day). We had decided we needed an event or two on Saturday to look organized and ready to go, so that was on me. The goal was to send the message that the NDP decision to force an election did not catch us off guard, and to show early momentum. Everyone else went to the bar on the basis of a commitment from a handful of staff that they would return and work with me to plan the next day. By nine p.m. no one had returned, and I began to worry. After a few phone calls and very direct discussions, I got the needed staff back into the room and we planned for the weekend and for Monday.

While the headquarters was basically ready to go, there were still a few significant things to tick off the list. The major issue was connectivity, as the internet and phones were not yet fully operational. It was of course everyone's expectation that everything would work perfectly from the get-go. It was a tense few days as we figured out the inconveniences and setbacks. Our brilliant operations manager Lesley Sherban worked tirelessly until we were functional but not without shedding a few tears from the pressure of those first forty-eight hours. Lesley's work ethic and intensity matched my own, and I would never have made it through that campaign without her. She's a good example of a staff person the campaign team would not have on board in 2018 because she'd chosen to move to Ottawa.

Lesson: Politics is cumulative. At some point in time, you will be given the chance to reach beyond anything you have ever done before. If you have control of the operation, there's no barriers to what you can do.

By the time the campaign began, I was in full control of the operation. I had painstakingly reviewed the plans of each department and we were in full execution mode. Of course, given that we had to be nimble and ready to respond to the opposition attacks, mistakes and even friendly fire, the HQ staff were carefully selected to maximize teamwork and ensure a smooth campaign effort.

I had moved into a state of mind that my family has long described as "campaign mode." There would nothing else that could have my time or energy.

Due to the Jewish holiday of Shavuot, the chief electoral officer recommended the campaign be extended by a week, making it a five-week campaign. It was up to the cabinet, but no government in its right mind would forego the recommendation of the CEO to avoid conflict with a religious holiday. It was also the right thing to do. David Herle was less than thrilled, as politically the extra week could prove problematic to momentum or even provide other campaigns the chance to catch up (we did end up fighting an NDP surge that last week). It also added to costs.

It was going to be a long campaign. Despite my love of dogs and kids, I set a rule that there would be no canine or human visitors to the central campaign headquarters. My own beloved Aussie shepherd, Nellie, spent the entire campaign, with the exception of one weekend, at the farm of our dog-walking company. I was working a minimum of sixteen hours a day, seven days a week, and it demanded my full energy. Distraction would work against a focused campaign that left no stone unturned. There was always a phone call to made or an email to be sent, so the culture was based on all work and no play.

It was on that basis that I made the decision to feed the team well and we had three good meals each day. Folks thanked me regularly that they were not subjected to a diet of just pizza and Chinese food. Of course, we had lots of that, too, but we had healthy food delivered daily both to avoid illness and to ensure staff could operate at their best. Okay, fine, it also kept people at their desks.

Bob Lopinski suggested to me that we have a morning meeting daily, at seven or seven thirty a.m., for the whole team. It would be an opportunity to update everyone before the day was overtaken by whatever issues would present themselves. Of greater interest to me, it would also get everyone to the office bright and early. Apparently, the approach had been used to great success in the McGuinty campaigns. I took the question to David, who had no problem but made it clear he'd never be seen at that hour. I have always been a morning person and was happy to take the helm and provide the daily updates. It worked out great—I would highlight successes of the previous day and talk about local campaigns, always thanking the team for their continuing efforts.

I believe that is what led Bob to describe the 2014 campaign as the most egalitarian and non-hierarchical campaign in which he'd ever participated. I was happy to hear that, because I'd worked hard to ensure people had the information they needed to lead their teams and understand what was happening in the campaign. I'd spent many campaigns working in the dark because the leadership would not share information. I found it frustrating and unfair when the real information was withheld, and we were told only positive news—even when the ground told us otherwise. Given the level at which this elite team was operating, they deserved the truth. Even bad news could be motivating if kept in the context of the overall campaign strategy.

There were a number of tough moments along the way. It is human nature to want to be in every important meeting but that is not often effective or efficient. Lots of people complained about too many meetings in the months leading up to the campaign, but it was so that we could have fewer during the campaign. I had hoped to have one meeting where the strategy for the next few days would be decided and those executing would get their marching orders directly.

It only took me a day or two to realize I had to separate those groups. The strategists and planners, while brilliant, tended to be free-wheeling, and it would sometimes take a while to get to a decision. Moreover, if they were in the room for discussions around execution, it would be seen as an opportunity for them to change their minds. I ultimately broke it into two meetings—one for planning and one for execution—and that process worked better and certainly allowed a much quicker turnaround in terms of the direction we were headed.

I provided strong leadership throughout the campaign. No one waited long for a decision. If the chain of command was broken because someone was busy with another issue (or even getting coffee), I'd provide the needed direction. There were some who chaffed at my hands-on approach as I reviewed every piece of paper that left the office and ensured the needed approvals were in place. In asking a few folks if I was micromanaging beyond what was appropriate, I was assured that without that level of control, the risk for error was too high. It was a fine balance between empowering the directors of each department to do their jobs and ensuring that the overall campaign ran like a well-tuned orchestra.

For me the 2014 campaign operated in the way I always believed a campaign could run, but rarely does. If you have ever stood in the middle of a large organization and felt it had a beating heart, you know what I mean. Done right, a campaign's heart can beat steady and strong. You can feel it. There is chaos and things happen every minute, but it's organized in a way to manage the impact of every nuance and change. Each person knows their role, the expectations, the needed short-term outcomes to achieve the very clear long-term goal. They know the heart of the effort and its brain are connected— passion and belief has to be matched by relentless hard work and dedication. People understand how their piece of the puzzle fits with the rest and that without their piece, it won't work.

That campaign had the hum of success. It was disciplined and the work came first. No one left until their part was done. Everyone pulled in the same direction. And I was at its head, loving every minute of the uncertainty, tension, fear and hope. I turned out the lights every night and I turned them on each morning.

Ten days before the end of the campaign, David informed me he was leaving the campaign office and joining the team on the bus. My immediate reaction was confusion and worry. I declared his idea as absurd and said he was needed at central campaign. David looked me in the eye and with a half-grin said firmly, "You have this. You are running this campaign and we're moving into the phase where the ground game takes over. I can do more by being on the bus with the leader." I felt scared, excited and honoured all at the same time. I had earned that moment, but I did not see it coming. And frankly, it had been a long time coming.

On June 12, 2014, we won a majority. The most satisfying headline I have ever read was on the front page of the *Toronto Star* the next morning: "Liberals defy all predictions of doom."

CHAPTER 7

The Politics of Survival

"Be courageous. It's one of the only places left uncrowded."
— ANITA RODDICK

In 2014, David Herle was able to develop a path for the miraculous election of a fourth straight Liberal government. His research was definitive: voters wanted change and this time, they meant it. Knowing that, he developed a thoughtful approach to convince the electorate that Kathleen Wynne was worthy of the chance to be that change.

Remember the "Never Stop" campaign ad? Kathleen Wynne in jogging gear running along a country road and up a hill, conveying thoughts about setting goals and never stopping until they are done. Many thought the ad was too risky. And yet it piqued the interest of media and voters. Kathleen was different by virtue of being a woman, and an openly gay woman at that. The non-traditional nature of the ad sent the message that she stood apart from the political pack.

I attended the focus groups who gave us feedback on the ad before it was released. Attendees were taken aback to see a premier in a somewhat unorthodox setting for an elected official. My favourite moment was when one fellow cracked, "She probably doesn't even run." Another man in the room snapped back saying, "Hey, I'm a jogger. And I can tell you that running up that hill is not easy." Exactly right. And exactly the reaction we wanted.

When voters took their leap of faith in June 2014, they made a choice, for the first time, to put a woman in charge. That confidence was grounded on the enormous expectation that the Liberal government would embody the same character and charisma the people had seen in the premier in the running ad and in the lead-up to the campaign. She looked and talked differently than the male leaders who had come before her; her government would be unlike the previous governments voters had come to despise.

Lesson: When you gain the confidence of the voters during an election, they have given you a gift. But between elections, that confidence is fragile and fleeting.

We'd been granted a stay of execution and it was up to us to do the most we could with our new lease on life, in the form of a majority government. Running a government with a woman at the helm afforded us the opportunity to take a very different direction, to strike out down a road intended to reflect the persona of Kathleen Wynne— caring, courageous, determined, outward-looking, inclusive. People believed she would be the person she herself described during the leadership campaign as "a social justice premier who would demonstrate a collaborative, fiscally responsible approach to governing."

It meant there was a real opportunity for measurable, structural change in government. Similarly, we could have addressed the organizational challenges we had long faced as a party and recovered some of the ground we had lost. But when you are the government, there is always some short-term problem or issue claiming your attention or considered more urgent. As a result, it's like you're talking about paint colours for your house while the foundation is crumbling, and you miss chances to make transformative change to the way things work.

In the end it seems the public's disappointment with the Wynne government was rooted in the reality that when the electorate leapt, there was no soft landing. Rather than immediately demonstrating that we could indeed change the way of things, we took the path most followed, falling into the usual patterns and operating the same as governments before us. While a majority mandate meant we could govern freely, making decisions we believed necessary and appropriate, it also meant high anticipation that problems would get solved. And in a province where for the first time the premier was a woman, there was a list of issues that specific groups believed would finally get attention. Others, who were detractors from the start, had concerns that a woman couldn't possibly understand the economy and feared a Kathleen Wynne Liberal government would put social policy ahead of fiscal policy. Underneath it all, though, was the ingrained belief that a woman would govern differently.

Lesson: Take the time to plan out the long game. The only way to stay ahead of the everyday stress is to have a road map to where you need to be before the next election.

It was heady stuff winning a fourth mandate in a row and the euphoria we felt took a while to wear off. I was full of excitement and hope. I understood my job was to oversee the politics of government. That meant I'd be the voice at the senior table who would represent the larger goals, the person who would keep an eye on the critical path to the next election and assess the political impact of every decision we made.

Along with being named deputy chief of staff, I requested and was given the title of chief operating officer. I didn't ask for that title for purposes of stature; it was to project authority. I'd always found that if you did not have the word "chief" in your title, particularly as a woman, it was much tougher to effect change and it was not unusual for people to try to work around you. It wasn't long after we began to function as a government that I realized I was up against a much bigger reality. Title alone was not going to automatically give me the clout I needed to bring about the disciplined approach I was known for.

The overarching challenge was convincing senior staff of the need to rise above the day-to-day pressure of governing and pay attention to the long-term strategy: what were our key goals as a government and what it would take to be re-elected? Four years would go by quickly. Good government (which I describe as delivering on what was expected of us and making sure the public knew it) was essential but it was never going to be enough to get us a fifth mandate. And while some argued we should position it as Kathleen Wynne's second mandate, in order to separate the McGuinty years from the Wynne years, that was never going to be the view of the general public. She led the Liberal Party and that party had been in charge since 2003, a significant amount of time for any modern-day government.

On that basis, I felt strongly that we needed to dig in from day one, leaving nothing to chance. We needed to act in a way that ensured the voters did not come to regret their faith in us. That meant the design and execution of a strategic plan, including concise messaging that the Liberal government was a force for good in their lives and one that projected hope for the future. More than anything, people needed to see the Kathleen Wynne who had stood with them during the December 2013 ice storm, as she went from shelter to shelter to check on folks. People suffering and away from their homes over the Christmas holidays saw a compassionate woman show up in person to be a witness to their circumstances and assure them her government was there to help.

In an op-ed written in response to the disapproval of the government's actions around the storm, Premier Wynne wrote, "I will not be constrained by the possibility that I will be criticized or that my political career may take a hit. I'm not in office to play it safe—I'm in office to do my best to help people." That is the Kathleen Wynne I knew, the woman who won us our reprieve. And had we continued to let that Kathleen Wynne be present in every decision of the government, I expect we would have fared much better.

Lesson: Always approach politics like you are in opposition. Be hungry and realize it can all slip away if you're not vigilant.

The win gave us four years to ensure the OLP was ready for 2018 and what would undoubtedly be the fight of our lives. Our voter base was not stable (as the middle rarely is) and we could not count on another poorly run Conservative campaign. The ground troops who had done the work in 2014 needed to remain engaged and active. We needed to raise enough money to allow for a sizeable level of pre-writ advertising and outreach. We needed to track our voter base and quickly react to any signal that they we were losing them. As a party and as a government, it would take a Herculean effort to be ready.

Everyone agreed with the theory of what was needed but the attempt to put it into practice proved quite a different story. Too much happens every day to throw you off course. But without a roadmap, you are left careening from side to side, bouncing off the latest urgent issue or crisis. You'll never get to where you need to be because you failed to map out the strategy.

Being in opposition is like being on the ropes every day. You're always looking at the long game—you're single minded and single hearted about getting elected. But sometimes after the win, when you're in government, the Centre starts to forget what it's like to have to fight, what it's like to have that kind of commitment to a cause.

When you find team members who understand this and are always hungry, you need to do all you can to get them to stay through to the political campaign sometimes years away. That alone can make or break a political organization.

I reached out to several key political staff and desperately tried to convince them to take a leave from their jobs in government and assume roles critical to the outcome of the election. I argued passionately. I begged. I got people more senior than me to make the outreach. Despite my efforts, I was unsuccessful.

It was then that I came to the realization of how different it was to learn about politics by being in opposition. How could there be any other priority than re-election?

Lesson: Push past the tendency in politics to assume that there is no option but to operate reactively. With discipline and an overarching set of goals, it is possible to create a proactive approach designed to measure every outcome against the set objectives.

I always believed that even in politics, you had to strive for the ideal. In the Wynne government, I found it far more elusive than I ever imagined possible.

We quickly fell into a way of acting that I refer to as "government-head" (meaning the work of the government is all we thought about). The premier's schedule was consumed by the demands of running a government. The circle around her was very tight from the start, with most of the advice flowing through Tom Teahan and Andrew Bevan. There were others who had a say and some input, usually on an issue-by-issue basis, but direct influence remained in the hands of a few. And I believe that resulted in a premier who was less than her best.

By early 2016 polling numbers started to show we were treading in rough waters. Even as our popularity began to falter, it was difficult to institute change over the approach. The premier's work effort was unmatched by any leader I'd ever known, with several meetings and events every day. But in the absence of a critical path that dictated how every outreach was meant to contribute to the desired long-term outcome (and even sometimes the short term), it was tough to regain the ground we were losing. We needed to capitalize on efforts by carefully assigning the premier's time. We needed to deploy a strong team behind her in the form of cabinet and caucus and maximize the outreach achieved through every point of contact.

I was the COO and therefore I take my share of responsibility for how things actually unfolded. But it became clear quite quickly that while I had the title, I did not have the authority to execute the role as I saw fit. A dotted line on the organization chart was meant to signal that every director reported to me operationally, but the reality was that with direct reporting relationships to Tom and Andrew,

many of the senior staff turned to them for the final say. This complicated my ability to establish a meticulous operational structure, and it
meant the question "Who's in charge?" was asked too often.

There was another reality that impacted my ability to take firm
control of the operations. It was only six months after starting in the
Premier's Office that I found myself under Ontario Provincial Police
(OPP) investigation. After my return from the Sudbury by-election,
there was a lot of general uneasiness. It would come and go but the
elephant in the room was always the investigation. It undermined
some of my authority and a lot of my self-confidence.

*Lesson: Capitalize on your best asset but do it with a plan and monitor
how it is going. Take nothing for granted.*

From the beginning, our greatest asset was Kathleen Wynne and she
was everywhere. But the downside of over-scheduling the person
everyone wanted to see was that the opportunity for a real connection was limited. Some argued attendance was enough. But rushing
her in and out said to people that she was there only as a politician;
the genuine woman they were there to meet—the woman in the running ad—was not in evidence. If she was in the room for three hours
but spent two of them at a head table, it was a missed opportunity.

I sought to address it by directing her tour staff to ensure the
schedule allowed the premier to linger for a while at the end of an
event or to be there early to greet people as they arrived. But often
by the time the final itinerary reached me, other meetings or small
events had made their way onto the schedule. It meant that too many
connections were fleeting and not at all meaningful—for the voter
and for the premier. As a result, people's views toward the accessible,
compassionate woman they thought they had elected were starting
to change. And not for the better.

There was an old-style view that it was not "premier-like" to have
the premier arrive early and greet guests. She should only enter to
a full room. Or that moving her from table to table during a meal

(to actually sit and talk with the people for up to twenty-minute intervals) was not appropriate. I argued on the basis that we had never sold Kathleen Wynne as "premier-like." People believed she was authentic and one of them. It's an area I wished I pushed harder to change. More so, I wish I had talked directly to the premier about it, as I believe she would have been more than okay with being visible to less people in exchange for an encounter having a lasting, positive impact.

External advisors constantly harangued us about getting outside of Toronto as often as we could. By getting the premier out on the road for a week straight, we could use every minute of the day to its maximum effect. It meant a slower pace, longer time with each person and sitting down with local media to talk about what mattered to the community she was visiting. Such outreach tours would start off with good intentions, but too often were derailed by a government event that people senior to me deemed critical. Time on the road would be cut back and we'd bring the premier back to Toronto to stand behind a podium or to fight a losing battle in the legislature.

The premier was the face of every major announcement, and many of the minor ones. Cabinet and MPPs would attend with her but we scheduled at least two or three announcements for the premier each week. We constantly argued over the value of travel versus staying close to Queen's Park so that the press gallery members would cover an announcement. I never understood the constant pressure to keep the gallery happy and the only response I ever got from the communications team was that I didn't understand the consequences of making them unhappy. I did understand, but *they* seemed to disregard the consequences of being focused on government only.

It felt like a vicious cycle. Instead of leaving downtown Toronto and missing question period, the premier would stay in the city for an announcement the press gallery would attend. Instead of going to even Hamilton or Aurora, we'd go three blocks down the street to the Metro YMCA at Grosvenor and Bay. We'd make the announcement and hurry back to the legislature for question period. If either question period or the scrums afterward yielded an issue of more interest to the press gallery, the intended impact would be lost. More often than not, an announcement that would have been front page on the *London Free Press* or the *Peterborough Examiner* got little or no coverage in a mainstream Toronto paper. To my political mind, it made no sense at all.

Getting the premier outside of the Queen's Park bubble had other benefits, including giving caucus members the opportunity to shine when the premier visited their ridings. It boosted the premier's spirits, which was critical to ensuring that the authentic Kathleen Wynne was always front and centre. It was golden because it was the premier at her best. As importantly, it was away from the whims of the gallery and the negative energy of question period. And politically, it made a local impact in a way nothing else could.

The only time I wasn't happy when the premier was out of the Centre was when she was on an international trip. Despite plummeting poll numbers, the premier was still taking trips that took her out of the country for up to a few weeks at a time. To me it was time better spent shoring up the troops or visiting ridings.

As the popularity of the leader and the party began to fade, there was a view that we needed to step back and assess what really mattered—and we needed to be cold-hearted about it. We did that a few times but only in a cursory way. And without a general at the helm with the authority to enforce the battle plan, "government-head" would take over again and we'd quickly fall back into the same old habits that just weren't working for us.

Lesson: A team is there to support the leader. Find their strengths, motivate them and put them to work.

One of the best resources of any government is the members of its cabinet and caucus. Working as a team and as an extension of the premier, they are positioned to make a substantial and sustainable impact on the both the success of government and the party brand.

That was not the way we worked. Caucus was a strong team, united behind their leader, but they were set apart from the Centre. Only a few (Deb Matthews, in particular, as deputy premier) were consulted on a regular basis.

MPPs and cabinet ministers operated fairly independently. In many cases, they learned about government announcements the night before or on the day they were made. Most issues brought to the cabinet table were quickly approved with little understanding of how they might fit into any larger plan. It felt like a series of independent, individual actions that did not reflect an overall approach toward re-election. Communications was discordant, superficial and rarely could we sustain a single good news issue for more than a day or two. Over time, caucus began to feel more and more removed from the decision-making process and from the direction of the government.

The partial privatization of Hydro One proved the best example of how we acted as a government first and a caucus and party second. Despite it being such a significant and unusual policy decision so off-brand for the Liberal Party, no polling had been done to see how the general public would respond to a mission-critical public entity being "sold off." There had been no effort to precondition voters in a way that they would understand the options before government in terms of having enough money to build much-needed infrastructure. We just announced it, without a real plan around how to communicate it.

When the announcement of the sale was made, people were in shock, internally and externally. Caucus was told about the plans late in the process and had no meaningful input, yet they were expected to go out and defend it. It was painful to hear caucus try to make sense of it themselves, let alone figure out how to convince their communities it was a sound economic decision.

The opposition successfully spun that privatization meant greater risk to our energy system and was directly responsible for the soaring hydro bills people received every month. Much of what was being said was not true, but our inability both to sell our plan and to push back on the views of the naysayers lost us serious support. The hydro issue was the single largest reason why our numbers began to fail as early as two years prior to the election, but why we did not recover from it was likely based in a much larger reality.

On the political side, my greatest worry was our failure to successfully engage with the ethnocultural communities. Caucus talked about it constantly and were rightly concerned about our ability to hold onto support in key groups. We assumed showing up at important events was sufficient to demonstrate to the communities that we cared. And that in return, they'd support us.

What we failed to do was develop a strategic plan that would lead to a meaningful relationship with each individual ethnocultural group. Communities once considered to be hardcore Liberal had been diversifying their support for a few decades. I knew a time, in Guelph in the late 1970s, when we pulled every single Italian family identified by long-time city alderman Mico Valeriote. I can still recall him sitting in the campaign office going through the voters lists and highlighting Italian voters. He'd skip over a few, saying they were not with us. We never canvassed them; we just knew that if Mico said so, they'd vote Liberal.

But those days were long gone. Using the Italians as an example, the next generation were as likely to vote Conservative or NDP as they were to vote Liberal. I noticed the vote shifting away from us when Laura Albanese ran in 2007, and in the Vaughan federal by-election against Julian Fantino in 2010. We did little to determine the root cause of it other than generational change resulting from improved economic status.

Like the rest of the voting population, voters from the more recent immigrant communities were concerned about the economy, health care, education and opportunities for their youth. But we needed to look beyond those mainstream issues to find what mattered to them as new immigrants to Canada—issues like family reunification, treatment of caregivers, home care for the elderly and language training for their children. Sometimes it was about the family they'd left behind or past wrongs they suffered in their home countries, particularly for those who arrived as refugees. Sometimes it was about racism and discrimination.

The leadership of many ethnocultural groups focused on ways to be part of the mainstream political process. They wanted MPPs that looked like them and understood the challenges they faced. That meant they needed to win nominations. The Scarborough Rouge River by-election in late summer 2016 showed me just how far behind we had fallen on this front. As the most diverse riding in the province, it gave me the opportunity to sit with the leadership of many of the ethnocultural groups. It was eye-opening as they talked about their high expectations of both government and the Liberal party, and the disappointment they were feeling. Meanwhile, the opposition was promising them the world with no thought whatsoever to what it would take to deliver on those commitments.

We failed to do the real work, which would have included acting to ensure government and the party reflected the diversity of our society. We needed to proactively recruit people from new immigrant communities to work in government, to be on local riding associations and to run for nominations. It meant truly engaging with the leadership. We needed to listen and really hear them. We needed to set goals and track the results. Instead we tended toward showing up at events, sending out cards in their own language or hosting a reception at Queen's Park. Those things had to be done but what communities wanted from us was a voice.

Politically, the story was the same. I realized while we were in Scarborough that we hadn't identified the leadership of specific communities to whom we could turn to for advice and support. We didn't have individual community members tagged in our database or a way to reach out to them in their own language. It was the kind of effort that had to be a priority all year around, not just in the lead-up to an election. We needed a large, committed team of staff rather than the small handful who weren't at the senior tables.

All that meant we were flying blind as to what it would take to keep the voters we had and how to grow the base by building bridges to a new group of voters who could be persuaded to back the Liberals. It just wasn't enough of a priority in our world and as a result, the support we traditionally counted on melted away.

We also needed to get the premier out of the cabinet room, the formal events and the boardrooms and into the living rooms. I've seen Kathleen Wynne at her best in those kinds of informal settings. That's where the real person always showed up. She didn't watch her words or hide her emotions, or avoid behaviour that might be perceived as uncertainty or weakness. In the Scarborough by-election we were in a three-way fight for the Tamil vote, and a senior person in the Hindu community, Ashwani Bhardwaj, brought a group of young Tamils into his home to meet with the premier.

Because it was a by-election, I was able to pull off the living room scenario given Ashwani's strong view that a family setting was best for what we needed to do. It turns out these young people had been delegates for Kathleen during her leadership and while they were delighted to see her again, they had a complaint. An earnest young man bravely told the premier that she'd let them down, reminding her that she'd agreed to meet with them after the leadership to talk about their issues as Tamil youth, but it had never been scheduled. In responding to their concerns, I saw the authentic, genuine Kathleen I knew and so did they. She apologized for having let them down and promised the meeting would happen. The atmosphere in the room brightened and they moved on to talk about issues relating to the larger community.

Lesson: What a voter looks for most is a genuine connection with a politician, to see them as someone who is real and who can understand what matters to the voter and why.

I remember the disconnection I felt when I would hear senior staff speak with the premier about how she was being perceived and as a result, how she should act in public. It left her second-guessing herself. Was she too shrill? Too forceful? Too meek? It seemed to me that such feedback was directly impacting her self-confidence at a time she needed it most. And that what we needed to do was find a way to empower Kathleen to always be her genuine self.

One of the first times I travelled with Kathleen was in November 2014 on a trip to Winnipeg. We toured the Canadian Museum for Human Rights and had a meeting with Manitoba premier Greg Selinger. But the primary purpose was to be the keynote speaker at a fundraising dinner for the Manitoba Liberal Party and its leader at the time, Rana Bokhari. There was some concern that as a premier, Kathleen Wynne was acting in a partisan manner by endorsing the Liberal party in another province, but as a political staffer, it made me proud to see her support a fellow woman Liberal leader.

When we stopped for lunch at an indoor market, I joined her at her table and started to chat away. At one point she said something like, "It's good to sit and talk. Usually I'm on my own." It was then that I realized none of the other staff were sitting with us, having chosen a spot a few tables away. I immediately apologized, thinking I must have been unaware of some protocol around her travel. She assured me it was never her idea, just that somehow it was assumed that staff should not sit with her because she was premier. I was in a bit of shock and it made me think a lot about the presumptions around how a premier is to act. In my world, a politician surrounded by people was always the better optics, and best for their well-being.

Upon our return, we were walking through Pearson International Airport. It was not unusual for people to approach the premier for photos or to say hello and when it happened, she was in her element. At one point a woman was moving quickly toward her saying, "Be prepared, I'm a hugger." I grinned as Kathleen dropped her luggage and replied, "That's okay because I'm a hugger, too." Watching them embrace made me think again about how to make it possible for the true Kathleen Wynne to emerge.

Frequently, it also would've been helpful to move the OPP security back several feet. Kathleen is a small woman and while doing their job, security can inadvertently block people's access to her. It was often in the large ethnic events that things could get intense as people tended to surge forward, looking to shake her hand or take a photo. When it was a political event, I'd often insert myself and lead the premier through the crowd because security generally gave me a little more leeway than the tour staff. But I also made it a practice to constantly make eye contact with the OPP, assuring them I knew the people around us and therefore there was no need to step in.

Perhaps the most moving Kathleen moment I witnessed was the night a plane arrived at Pearson carrying the first group of Syrian refugees who would settle in Canada. It was proving quite a logistical challenge since the plane was expected to arrive close to midnight and security was intense given that Prime Minister Justin Trudeau would lead the welcoming committee. At the last minute, my sixth sense kicked in and I decided to show up. I'm glad I did—both to support the premier and because of what I got to be a part of, as a proud Canadian.

When I got there, it was clear to me that nobody had given any thought to where the premier would wait for the plane's arrival. I approached the tour lead for the prime minister, Adam Grech, and asked if it would be okay for the premier and our small group to wait at the PM's waiting area, too. He graciously agreed. I knew the premier was nervous about the event, but she immediately relaxed as Prime Minister Trudeau arrived and they took the opportunity to chat freely about several issues. I overheard her getting advice from defence minister Harjit Sajjan about the lobby to exempt members of the Sikh community from wearing helmets while riding a motorcycle. She was in her element.

As we moved out of the waiting area to greet the refugees, Kathleen thanked me for being there, saying, "I always feel that when you are here, nothing can go wrong." I appreciated the comment, more than she knew. It was incredibly moving to watch Kathleen during the arrival of the refugees. The interaction was only with families who made the choice to stop and talk. It was heart-wrenching to hear small kids and parents describe their experiences and more importantly, how relieved and happy they were to be on solid ground in Canada. Some talked of feeling safe for the first time in a very long time. Kathleen held their hands and just listened.

At one point I looked to my left to see then-immigration minister John McCallum and Minister Sajjan sitting on the ground surrounded by a group of kids. They were helping them repack what few personal possessions they were carrying with the new belongings they had been given upon arrival. It was such a special night.

The kids were a mixture of excitement and exhaustion. Because it was December, at one of the stops the refugees were being outfitted with winter clothing. The premier and the PM helped kids try on jackets and hats. I heard the premier ask one little girl if she liked her new coat, focusing on the fit. The little girl replied that she did and then shyly whispered, "Could I have a pink one?" I saw the tears leap into Kathleen's eyes as she responded, "Of course you can have a pink one." She moved quickly to find one in the same size and she and the little girl beamed at their success. The premier and the PM were oblivious to the cameras around them as they focused on the very real, heart-warming moments unfolding before them, knowing government had done a heroic thing.

That was the Kathleen who cared, who loved people for who they were and could look beyond their differences to focus on what made them alike. This outlook also applied to her colleagues in the legislature. Kathleen could be a hardcore partisan, but she always treated other MPPs with respect and given the chance, would count them as friends. It was always sad to witness the unfriendly and unkind exchanges that would happen between MPPs in the legislature and on social media.

I'd always had a cordial relationship with Tim Hudak, the former Progressive Conservative leader we'd defeated in 2014. He resigned as MPP in August 2016 to move into the private sector as CEO of the Ontario Real Estate Association. On the day of his going-away party I ran into him in the hallway and he invited me to drop by. He added, "And bring Kathleen," never believing for a minute that I would. Later that afternoon I came across the premier waiting to head out to an event. I stepped into the premier's office and threw out the suggestion, saying that if she would go, I would go too (keep in mind I was under OPP investigation and seeing us together would generate chatter).

She immediately said yes and while it confused a number of staff, off we went. Our arrival caused a ripple in the room. PC leader Patrick Brown stood nearby, refusing to acknowledge our presence. Tim was thrilled and he had a lovely visit with Kathleen. TVOntario anchor and journalist Steve Paikin tweeted there was still some honour left among colleagues in the legislature. To me, this was who Kathleen was and I knew she would have wanted to give Tim her best. As we left, he handed me a postcard. On the back it read, *Thanks for coming by to make sure I really was gone.*

CHAPTER 8

When All Else Fails, Stay Focused and Work Hard

"You gain strength, courage and confidence by every experience
in which you really stop to look fear in the face. You must do the
thing you think you cannot do."
– ELEANOR ROOSEVELT

For close to three years, I was investigated, charged and made
to stand trial for an action I'd taken on behalf of the Ontario
Liberal Party. It was a charge later proven to be unwarranted and
unfounded. But regardless of its lack of merit, the very exercise was
a turning point in my life and career. At the time, I was in the campaign director role as a volunteer, and my day job was deputy chief of
staff to the premier of Ontario.

Almost from day one, the debate around the Sudbury by-election
was intense and convoluted. Political spin took over the facts and
with investigations underway, it was tough to set the record straight.
Until the whole story came out nearly two years later, during the
trial, it was presumed something nefarious had taken place and was
looked upon with immense intrigue. In reality, the story around the
recruitment of Glenn Thibeault as the Liberal candidate unfolded
similarly to the way all candidates are recruited. The big difference
was that Glenn switched parties to run and that the past candidate
decided to act solely in his own self-interest and in a way unexpected
of a partisan.

On November 19, 2014, right around noon, I ducked into the cabinet room and headed straight to Premier Wynne. I was anxious to share the news that Joe Cimino, an NDP MPP elected for the first time in the general election held only six months earlier, had just stood up in the legislature and resigned his seat for personal reasons, effective immediately. We were having a by-election and it would take place in Sudbury—the only previously Liberal riding we'd lost in the 2014 campaign and one where the local riding dynamic was less than ideal.

There was genuine excitement around the news, but we needed to move quickly on when to call the by-election and who would be our candidate. We knew we had been handed a gift and there was unanimous agreement it was a priority to win back the riding. It had been held for nineteen years by a well-liked Liberal, Rick Bartolucci. Although we lost the riding to the NDP in the general election by just 980 votes, it was clear the Liberal base was still strong. There was a consensus to go as quickly as possible. We decided we'd call it on January 7 and hold the by-election on February 5.

So we knew the when and the how, but we didn't know the who. We hadn't landed on a candidate. The day after Cimino's resignation, our past candidate Andrew Olivier declared over social media that he would be seeking the nomination. But everyone on the call agreed that Andrew was not our ideal candidate. In 2014, he'd been unwilling to take advice from the Centre or long-time local Liberals and frankly, he'd lost.

We agreed Vince Borg, who had co-chaired our province-wide candidate search committee leading up the 2014 election, would quickly explore our options. We still knew it was highly likely Andrew would be our candidate. But we wanted to be sure we did our due diligence. If we somehow found a star candidate in such a short time, we'd use the leader's power to appoint.

After making a series of calls, Vince advised the only person showing interest in running was again Marianne Matichuk, the former mayor. Marianne felt that if we gave her a few weeks, she could sell enough memberships to be competitive with Andrew.

Ultimately the Centre determined that the imperative was to hold the by-election as quickly as possible and as such, we'd be fine with Andrew as our candidate.

Lesson: Very little is as straightforward as it seems. Behind the scenes, the chess pieces are constantly being moved.

I arranged for a meeting to be set up for me to speak with the executive of the riding association. I had also asked for key local Liberals to be there, including Dr. Rayudu Koka, who headed the Sudbury Multicultural Council, and Gerry Lougheed, a senior Liberal advisor and local fundraiser. The goal was to put the general election issues behind us and develop a plan to win. The meeting was tense, but Gerry and I agreed it had gone well. Once it was over, we were excited to have a chance to talk about a new development that had come to light in the previous twenty-four hours: Glenn Thibeault, the federal NDP MP for Sudbury, was possibly interested in switching parties and levels of government to stand as our candidate.

I'd heard the name Glenn Thibeault for the first time just two days before. I'd received an email from Pierre Cyr, the director of operations in the Premier's Office and the OLP vice-president organization. He'd been making some calls in the francophone community around Sudbury to get their input. He sent me an email late in the day on November 24, stating he'd had a conversation with Domenic Giroux, then president of Laurentian University but previously an assistant deputy minister at the Ministry of Education when Kathleen Wynne had been minister. It was through Domenic that we learned of Glenn's possible interest, albeit a long shot.

The next day, everyone including the leader decided we'd pursue the long shot. It would be tricky given he was an NDP MP. I called Gerry and asked him what he thought. Gerry advised he had from time to time talked with Glenn about becoming a Liberal federally and had gotten nowhere. But it was a game-changer if we could get him. Gerry contacted Glenn and arranged a breakfast for that Friday morning. Leaving the next steps to Gerry, I continued to plan on the basis that Andrew would be our candidate.

That Friday, against the odds and considering everything that would come with the decision to defect from the NDP, Glenn told Gerry he was prepared to consider it. We agreed the next step would be for Glenn to meet Premier Wynne, whom he'd long admired but had never met in person. I called Glenn and set up a call between them, learning he'd be in Toronto that weekend. On Friday afternoon, the premier called Glenn and told him she'd be thrilled to talk with him about becoming our candidate.

That Sunday morning, November 30, I picked up Glenn at his hotel and drove him to the premier's home. The three of us met for close to an hour. They had an immediate connection, chatting about every issue they had in common, but eventually I focused them on the question at hand—what would it take to get Glenn to run for us? There was the expected discussion about the role Glenn would play in the Liberal government.

Wanting to manage expectations from the beginning, the premier called me prior to the meeting to discuss how best to handle things. She told Glenn that a cabinet position was not on the table, explaining that in her approach to naming cabinet, no one in their first term got in. She assured him she needed him at the caucus table and that eventually he could earn his way into cabinet. It was a minor part of the overall discussion that morning.

Glenn had only one real concern—that he could win the riding. He was going to be required to take an incredible leap of faith, and it was understandable he needed assurances we'd step up. His people were NDP organizers and many would be furious with him. He'd need the local Liberal team on board but given past experience, we could not count on how they'd react. More than anything, he seemed to need an assurance that Sudbury really did matter to us. We already had a majority, so would we really fight full-out to win what ultimately was just another riding?

The premier assured Glenn that in her view, there was no such thing as "just another riding." Sudbury should never have been lost and she wanted it back. I assured him that the Centre would run a professional, fully funded and organized campaign, and that we'd deliver him a win. Toward the end of the meeting, the premier told Glenn that if he was willing to run for us, she wanted him to be our candidate. The premier assured him that should she need to clear the way, she would use her power as leader to appoint the candidate.

We discussed the impact on Andrew. While the OPP were later determined that our focus must have been how to "manage" Andrew, this discussion had been in the context of how upset he would be and that as a past candidate, he was a valued member of the party. Glenn considered him a friend and felt he'd be supportive. There was a shared desire to keep him involved and to help him through what would be a disappointing reality.

Glenn asked the premier for a week to get to a decision, but I felt he might need a little longer. I was determined to give Glenn the time he needed. My biggest worry was that if we pressured for an answer, we might end up with "No." Glenn and I talked many times between November 30 and December 11. Essentially in those ten days, Glenn contemplated blowing up his world. Glenn was a Jack Layton guy but no longer believed in the NDP under Tom Mulcair. He was tired of the commute to Ottawa and was still physically suffering from the consequences of a major car accident that previous winter.

He was miserable given the time away from his wife and two young daughters and had been staggered by the very recent terrorist attack on Parliament Hill. When I told him that the Ontario legislature does not sit on Fridays, he was excited at the thought of having a day a week dedicated to constituency work and an extra day at home with his family. He would be taking a major pay cut and he'd forego his severance by quitting mid-term. He'd also built important relationships within the NDP.

Along with everything else, Glenn was aware of what would happen by switching parties. He'd be called a traitor, an opportunist and a

CHAPTER 8

liar. He'd be causing the taxpayers to pay for a federal by-election. The attack on his person would be swift and intense. And there would be consequences for those around him. Methodically Glenn worked through it all. I was genuinely impressed that much of his concern was for his staff, and told him so. Eventually he got to the point where the pros out-weighed the cons. I was mainly a sounding board and the only real assurance I gave him day after day was that we would win the riding. I knew by-elections and I was confident we could deliver the win, in no small measure due to his personal popularity.

On December 11, I was in our morning senior staff meeting when a number flashed across my phone. I realized it was Glenn and glanced at the premier, who seemed to know instantly I needed to take the call. I stepped into the hallway and called him back. Glenn stated he would need more time but as I took a deep breath, he laughed and said, "Sorry, bad joke... I'm in," followed by, "Let's do this." I pulled the premier out of the meeting, giving Glenn the chance to tell her directly. It was an exhilarating moment: we had landed our star candidate.

Glenn and I talked again later that day. With a lot whirling around his mind, he made one troubling request: could we hold the announcement of his candidacy until after Christmas, so he could enjoy the holidays with his family before all hell broke loose? It was one of the things that endeared me to Glenn right from the beginning. He wanted to focus on giving his kids a wonderful Christmas and not have them exposed to ugly comments from the public and media. I thought that timing was next to impossible but replied that we'd do all we could.

The next issue was what to do about Andrew and Marianne. Both had started their campaigns. Marianne as the past mayor, and Andrew as the past candidate, could be embarrassed by the need to walk back their decisions to run. Gerry insisted that Andrew and Marianne be told that very day. He felt confident both would accept that Glenn's stature in the community made him the best candidate, and would step back. Glenn, too, felt confident they would back him.

Gerry believed they would keep the information confidential until we were ready to announce.

Somewhat against my better judgement, I supported Gerry's decision to talk to Andrew and Marianne that day. As it turns out, it was the biggest mistake of my political life. Marianne acquiesced saying that if that was the decision of the premier, she would abide by it. She'd be happy to support Glenn. At four p.m. that same day, Gerry held an in-person meeting with Andrew in Andrew's office. I knew Gerry was going to discuss several options with Andrew, to keep him involved in the campaign, including acting as a campaign co-chair.

Gerry called me immediately after to say it had not gone well. With the Liberal caucus Christmas party well underway in the caucus offices, I needed a quiet place to talk with Gerry. I went into the photocopy room and closed the door. It didn't help much with the noise, but I got enough from Gerry to understand that he was unsuccessful in his mission to get Andrew to step aside and support Glenn as the candidate. He felt it essential that the premier make a call to Andrew that evening to reinforce his message.

I phoned Andrew and acknowledged he must be reeling from the news but explained that Premier Wynne hoped to talk with him. He was in the car on his way home and said he'd need a few minutes to get inside and set up (I later came to understand the words "set up" in a very different way). I pulled the premier away from the staff party and into Azam Ishmael's LCSB office. We debriefed quickly but the premier already knew what she wanted to say to Andrew. She had suggested earlier that she be the one to break the news, as she could identify with the disappointment he would feel, and felt as leader it was her role to be part of the message. She called from a landline. As it was so noisy, we were unable to use the speaker phone, so I could only monitor her side of the call.

She walked Andrew through her reasons and her vision and stated that Glenn would be the candidate. She took responsibility for the decision. At one point I heard her say something along the lines of "I know you will be mad, and it's okay to be mad. But it's me you should be mad at." Premier Wynne acknowledged how much she was asking of him. She took the time to outline her own experience with the party having a preferred candidate over her. She told him she had made the decision she felt best for Sudbury and for the party.

Some people asked me why I would ever have involved the premier in the discussions with Andrew. And it's a fair question. She told it best herself during her interview with the OPP. She called Andrew to provide emotional support as the leader asking someone to do something she knew was tough, and that would put him in difficult circumstances. She acted as the kind of leader she aspired to be. Toward the end of the call, the premier's tone became a little more edgy. I heard her say, "I hope you will accept my decision, as I would prefer not to have to use the appointment process."

I heard from Andrew early the next morning, in a text, asking for a call later in the day. We set it for five p.m. Andrew opened the call by saying that having given it thought and after consulting with advisors, he intended to seek the nomination. I was taken aback that, given what the premier had said to him, Andrew would think this route was even an option. I wanted to give Andrew the benefit of the doubt as it had only been thirty-six hours since he received the news. I decided to focus on the human being who was clearly still absorbing the idea that the party did not want him back as the candidate.

Deb Matthews, then deputy premier, addressed caucus the day the taped conversation was released. She encouraged everyone to listen to the recording, stating, "You will hear a much kinder, gentler Pat Sorbara than you are used to." She was right. Those who know me knew that while I was more than capable of shutting Andrew down, I was motivated by wanting to support him as a person.

As the next step, Andrew said he'd like to talk with Glenn. I was happy to facilitate the meeting, knowing Glenn wanted to talk with him; they were friends and he wanted to ask for Andrew's support directly. When Andrew lost in 2014, Glenn took the time to visit Andrew the next day, making sure he was doing okay. When Andrew mentioned he felt being mentored by Glenn would be a great opportunity for him, it gave me hope he was moving forward and would stay in the Liberal family. At the end of the call I suggested other avenues of involvement for Andrew in such a context, including work at the constituency office, a possible appointment to a board or commission, or a position on the executive.

There was absolutely no doubt in my mind that Andrew would be an excellent person to be appointed to a board or to work with the party. He met many of the key characteristics needed in the effort to create a more diverse and representative set of appointees. Andrew is a northerner, a francophone and a businessperson. And as a quadriplegic (he'd been injured during a hockey game and had been in a wheelchair since age fourteen), he would bring the voice of the disabled community. It was a no-brainer for me to talk about the opportunities available in government because he was such a good fit. We would have been lucky to have him in any of the roles we discussed.

Lesson: Honesty is the best policy, no matter where you work, but in politics it can lead to greater consequences.

In any situation, political or otherwise, you have to consider the context. Though many believed my outreach was motivated by something more sinister than kindness or generosity, it is precisely why I handled the call the way I did, instead of just shutting Andrew down. I wanted to help him face his disappointment by making sure he knew he still had a future in politics, should he want one.

In reflecting back on this, I thought about something I learned when working with Gordon Ashworth. I was Gordon's executive assistant when he was executive director of the Office of the Premier. In 1985, after the initial round of hiring, there were around six hundred people ecstatic at the opportunity to work as political staff in the brand-new Peterson government. There were hundreds more disappointed. Many did not give up and would seek to meet with Gordon to discuss how to get a job. Those who had worked for the party as volunteers for a long time had difficulty understanding that their loyalty and hard work was not going to result in the reward of a job or an appointment.

Gordon was not always one to give a direct answer, so it would leave folks with a bit of hope. Most people would eventually get the message and give up. But others would keep coming back. They'd tell me Gordon had signalled something would open up for them, if they would just be patient. I knew otherwise, and it was incredibly tough to watch people lose heart as they waited and waited. I believed they deserved to be treated with respect and fairness. In my mind, that meant an honest conversation.

One day, after a long-time Liberal had literally sat on the couch outside of our offices for three days hoping for a quick word with Gordon, I went out and laid it on the line. There would be no job. I explained that sometimes the skills you learn from campaigning don't necessarily translate into the skills you need in government. In other situations where it was more personal, I'd explain that, too. Did I ever regret telling someone the truth? Not often. I became known quickly as someone who would give you the straight goods. And that's the way I was treating Andrew when I spoke with him about the Sudbury by-election.

Straight-up conversations have consequences. Some people would thank me for being honest and helping them deal with reality. They went away and worked hard to improve their chances at a job in future. Others choose to believe I had denied them a job and carried grudges through many years.

At the end of the day, it was not relevant to me what Andrew decided he wanted to do, nor was it my view that he needed to be managed. By the time I spoke with him, Glenn was our candidate, he would be appointed if needed, and the campaign was moving forward. It was clear that many voters in Sudbury believed in Glenn as an individual, which proved to be a darn good thing given it was the primary reason we were able to overcome the challenges of the next several weeks and win the by-election.

After my call with Andrew, I updated the group to say I thought it had gone well. The conversation had been open, honest and civil, at least on my part. Andrew was calm throughout and seem engaged in the discussion. He portrayed no sense of betrayal or upset. There was disappointment, for sure, but nothing suggested he'd take any action to hurt the party. Glenn called me after his meeting with Andrew on Saturday morning. He felt good that they'd had a chance to talk. He said Andrew was very determined and did not give an answer when Glenn asked for his support. Instead, Andrew advised Glenn he needed the weekend to think about things and talk to his advisors. I sent a follow-up text to Andrew that day, saying I was around all weekend if he wanted to talk. I offered him another opportunity to speak with the premier. I never again heard from Andrew.

On Monday morning, December 15, a few people let me know Andrew announced on Facebook that he was having a press conference at ten a.m. I texted and called him at least three times, but he did not respond. My last text said the following: "Whatever you have decided, I hope you would show the premier the same courtesy that she has shown you and advise her in advance of your decision, whatever that is." I never heard back. Instead of letting anyone in the OLP know of his decision, Andrew met with the media to say he was withdrawing as a candidate for nomination.

Andrew told the media that he wasn't wanted, that the OLP had made a different choice. Likely out of respect for their friendship but maybe because Glenn was local and not the Centre, Andrew did not give Glenn's name to the media. Without Glenn's name, the focus was on Andrew. The immediate response was sympathy for poor Andrew, the past candidate who had worked so hard and come so close.

Of all that he said, Andrew's statement that, "I will not be bullied, I will not be bought" threw me the most. It was the first indication that he intended to misconstrue what we had discussed. But I had a job to do and couldn't worry about anything other than managing the next steps around Glenn's candidacy. We would be lucky if we got through the day without his name being leaked.

The biggest issue was Glenn had not yet told all of his family (specifically his one-hundred-year-old father), nor had he formally told Tom Mulcair. There had been one discussion between Glenn and Tom where Glenn signalled he was considering running in the by-election. Glenn assumed Tom believed it would be for the NDP, but he hadn't asked. On top of that, Glenn had resigned his position as national caucus chair the week before, so it likely wasn't a total surprise.

By the end of day, the *Toronto Star* had Glenn's name, apparently shared by the NDP. Robert Benzie was good enough to give us the night to get ready, saying he'd hold the story for the morning as long as we gave him the exclusive. It was a good deal and we took it. The next morning we put out a press release indicating Glenn would be our candidate. The reaction to Glenn was positive but at the same time, we immediately began fighting the rearguard reaction of the NDP, who were incensed by the defection.

In immediate response to Andrew's press conference, NDP House leader Gilles Bisson sent a letter to Ontario chief electoral officer Greg Essensa suggesting an investigation was required under the *Election Act*. And subsequent to PC House leader Steve Clark sending a letter to OPP commissioner Vincent Hawkes, the OPP announced they were going to undertake a criminal investigation into potential offences under sections 121 and 125 of the Criminal Code of Canada.

With the help of Derek Lipman, regional assistant for the north for the LCSB, we circled the wagons as quickly as we could with local Liberals. We knew Rick Bartolucci was far more critical to the outcome of the by-election than Andrew would ever be. When I spoke to local riding president Bill Nurmi, he was none too pleased about how he found out, but he was impressed with Glenn being the candidate. Rick was on board with Glenn but dismayed at how he felt the local executive was being treated.

That Friday, December 19, Premier Wynne and I headed to Sudbury. Our first stop was Rick's home, as he and his wife Maureen hosted a meeting of the local executive. There had been rumours of a mass resignation but regardless of the action they'd decided to take, we owed them an apology and an explanation. Glenn was not included, as this was between the riding and the Centre. This meeting was Kathleen Wynne at her best. She was her genuine, authentic self. She felt bad and didn't try to hide it. She told them she worried about the relationship we'd had in the past with the executive, as well as why she decided to appoint Glenn and how losing Sudbury in the general election had made her feel.

As the folks in the room listened, their affection for her as a person was evident. They told her openly how they felt in the lead-up to the general election and now. They talked about being left out of Andrew's 2014 campaign, with their years of experience and commitment seemingly deemed to have no value. It was a rare political moment of a leader having an honest exchange with her local team.

It was a moment of realization for me. The relationship between the Centre and the riding should never have been allowed to disintegrate to that degree. In the lead-up to 2014, we'd gone to our corners, entrenched in our positions, and stopped communicating except through the media. The result was that instead of uniting behind a cause, we were searching for a way to work together. I assured them that we wanted them all involved, and I meant it. I also took the opportunity to apologize and to let them know we had every intention of telling them ahead of the media, but because of Andrew's unexpected announcement we'd lost control of the timeline.

Lesson: Keep your eye on the ball, personally and professionally. The higher you rise, the deeper the muck, and you have to learn to manage your way through it.

Throughout the holidays, we focused on getting up and running. Landon Tresise accepted the role of campaign manager and was taking over control of the day to day. The imperative was to find a headquarters, recruit the team (which would be comprised of staff who would take a leave and/or vacation from their day jobs at the party or in government) and lodging for both the full-time staff and the hundreds who would be coming from Toronto to canvass on weekends.

On January 5, Andrew announced he would be running in the by-election as an independent. At that point, it was not a surprise. While the media wrote stories trying to suggest Andrew could win, there was no chance that was going to happen. I was in Toronto but held calls twice daily with the team in Sudbury. I pushed them hard. They were doing an excellent job, but I felt the need to be sure that nothing slipped because of the local intrigue.

As campaign manager, Landon's job became keeping Glenn focused and calm. He provided personal support to a candidate who was already facing so much pressure because of his defection from the NDP. I remained in the "bad cop" role, driving the campaign to get the work done. Landon moved into the "good cop" role, keeping the full-time folks engaged and helping them through their angst. He excelled at talking Glenn through every moment of uncertainty, and a true friendship emerged.

On January 12, 2015, the OPP announced they had examined the allegations made by Andrew and concluded there was no criminal offence committed. We learned that part of their decision was related to the fact that Andrew had refused to give them tapes he had recorded of our phone conversations. As a result, the media put pressure on Andrew to release them, which he did on January 15.

I listened to the tapes for the first time with director of issues management Brian Clow from the Premier's Office, who indicated he could see no problem. Our view was the tape vindicated me, in that Andrew had been neither been bullied or bought. But the by-election provided a perfect storm. The story stayed front and centre and was viewed in as negative a light as possible. The OPP reopened the criminal investigation and Elections Ontario indicated they'd be undertaking an investigation in response to the complaint received from Gilles Bisson.

Despite the controversy swirling, I headed to Sudbury for the last nineteen days of the by-election. It was clear to me that I needed to be on-site to drive the campaign. On top of everything else, losing the by-election would be a disaster—indicating that our decision to appoint a star candidate over the past candidate was a mistake. Our belief was that with a strong campaign, voters would elect Glenn, the best person to represent their riding.

Despite being in the midst of a by-election, I received a demand that I submit to a voluntary interview by Elections Ontario investigators, or face a subpoena. Chief elections officer Greg Essensa refused to delay the interviews despite the fact he knew everyone was focused on the by-election.

The CEO's decision to undertake and complete his investigation during the by-election provided a basis on which the highly partisan activity already underway would break wide open. Opposition politicians and the media focused on the investigations underway by both the OPP and the CEO, to the exclusion of almost all else.

The day of my interview I was exhausted and anxious. Beyond working fourteen-hour days on the by-election, Elections Ontario had demanded I provide all relevant emails and notes. Based on their list of keywords, I was instructed to undertake a search on all emails (government, OLP and home) and to provide relevant information, as well as any written notes, prior to my interview. Even with technical help, it took me two all-nighters.

Lesson: If you are going to work in politics, you need to be able to put your emotions aside and focus on getting the job done. There's always time for crying later.

During the interview, I was asked what I would call cursory questions. There was no attempt to probe the full context of the decision to move forward with Glenn as our candidate. There were no questions about my intentions, motivation, how my experience dictated my actions or my overall goal in talking with Andrew. While those issues appeared irrelevant to Elections Ontario, they made all the difference in the trial.

Deep down I knew we had made a dreadful mistake. Without any pushback, we accepted the process forced upon us by Elections Ontario, using a section that had been added to the *Election Act* five years earlier but never before used. My lawyer Bill Trudell later confirmed to me that had he been brought in sooner, he likely would have taken the position that the steps taken by EO were highly prejudiced and would directly impact future proceedings. Certainly, he would have demanded enough time to ensure his client was ready to be interviewed. It had become clear that the entire focus of EO's investigation was to produce a report on time for the start of the legislature in February.

When I returned from my interview I found Gerry sitting in his vehicle, outside of the campaign headquarters, waiting for me. He told me the OPP had reached out to him and he'd voluntarily attended an interview at their offices that afternoon, without legal counsel. In some shock, I asked him why he would have done that. He told me he had nothing to hide and felt that being cooperative was a way to demonstrate he'd done nothing wrong. Shaking my head, I said, "I have to now go and call my legal counsel and tell him what you've done."

I then checked my emails and there it was. A request from Detective Sergeant Shawn Evans from the OPP Anti-Rackets Branch, Corruption Unit, asking to set up an interview. Glenn had heard from him as well, asking to see him as soon as possible. At Tom Teahen's direction, I reached out to defense attorney Bill Trudell who that day became my lawyer. Bill took over contact with the OPP and indicated to them there would be no interview prior to the end of the by-election; he'd need time to get up to speed and to ensure his client was ready for any interview.

The by-election itself was going well. The team responded to the adversity by pulling together. There was no need to explain the imperative to win. Waves of staff came up from Queen's Park to canvass, as did Liberals from across the province. Landon helped Glenn to manage his anxiety while I kept him focused on staying at the doors, asking for votes. He worked incredibly hard, canvassing in some of the worst weather I had ever seen. Premier Wynne made seven trips to the riding, far more than normal. Fighting on a number of levels, her presence helped Glenn and buoyed the troops.

February 5 dawned and we were ready to go, having dominated the ground war throughout the byelection. Late in the morning of election day, the media released the contents of the OPP's Intent to Obtain (ITO) order, in relation to their investigation into possible criminal charges. News stories started in the early afternoon and in today's world of social media, spread like wildfire. That afternoon, director of communications Rebecca Mackenzie called me to say I would have to avoid the celebration that evening. The place would be crawling with media and the decision had been made not to comment on the scandal. Politically I understood the decision but emotionally it was tough. For the first time that day, the tears flowed. After everything we'd gone through, it was demoralizing to not be able to celebrate getting Glenn over the finish line.

Lesson: What's asked of you in politics is not always fair, but true partisans put the party first.

I stayed in the campaign office as the votes were counted and relayed the numbers through Landon to Glenn and the premier, who were gathered in a suite at the Holiday Inn. Although I knew we'd won, Glenn did not want to declare victory until it was confirmed by the media. I headed over to the hotel to convince him in person. As I walked along the gangway to the suite, I realized I was walking above the room where around four hundred people who'd come from across the province to pull vote were gathered to watch the results and celebrate. I offered a thumbs up to a few folks who had spotted me, feeling sad I could not join them. A group of staff had turned toward me and were chanting my name. Eventually the entire room was cheering and chanting. I gave them a wave, put my hand on my heart, and continued to the suite. My spirits soared and much of the grime of the day washed away.

As I entered the suite, I hugged the premier and then Glenn. I assured him he'd won and told him he needed to get down to the party, join his team and celebrate his victory. Rebecca decided I could trail behind, given that the media would be watching the premier and Glenn. I was able to see their speeches before returning quickly to the suite. With everything that had happened, winning that by-election was critical. At the very least, and regardless of what was to come, we had earned that celebration.

But from December 15, 2015, when Andrew held his press conference until I was charged on November 1, 2016, it felt like a cloud had descended on my life and followed me everywhere. Some days that cloud was light grey and other days it was downright black. Friends and the leadership in the OLP and the Premier's Office stood by me fully, at least at the beginning of it all.

CHAPTER 9

You Serve at the Pleasure of the Leader

"There are people who take the heart out of you, and there are
people who put it back."
  – Elizabeth David

We won the by-election on February 5 and the legislature re-
sumed on February 17. The Thursday of that week was a horrible day. CEO Essensa lobbed a grenade in the form of his report to
the legislature, which he provides following every by-election. "The
Chief Electoral Officer's Report on Apparent Contraventions of
the *Election Act*" was presented to the speaker and distributed to the
members at the start of daily proceedings, only a few minutes before
question period began. While we had been made aware of its general content the night before, we were not given the courtesy of an
advance copy. The premier was therefore pretty much left to fend for
herself when the assault from the opposition started.

Our issues management team read quickly through the report
and called attention to the CEO's statement that he was not in the
position to determine guilt or innocence. Although it got worked
into the answers, it didn't really help based on the CEO's overall con-
tention that actions taken by Gerry and me "may" have contravened
the *Act*. It was all the opposition needed to throw the presumption
of innocence out the window, publicly declare us guilty and demand
resignations.

Later that day I sat in the Premier's Office with the premier and Tom Teahen. Andrew Bevan was on the phone. I was in the position no political staff person ever wants to be in: I had become the story. The media and opposition were firm that I had to resign given the CEO's report, as it would almost certainly lead to an OPP investigation. I took the only step left open to me as a senior member of staff and through tears, voice shaking, I offered my resignation. Tom and Andrew felt strongly we should avoid the tendency toward a knee-jerk reaction. The premier acknowledged she may have no choice but to accept it, but she decided she needed to think about it. She had to consider the overall impact on the government and her brand.

Lesson: You don't know what it means to "serve at the pleasure of the leader" until you're called to do so. When you're at a crossroads, you may have little choice but to fall on your sword.

I left the Premier's Office not knowing if I'd ever step foot in it again. In the end, she took the risky path. Instead of throwing me under the bus, we boarded it together and with the caucus and the party, buckled our seatbelts and braced for impact. On February 20, 2015, Premier Wynne woke up at four a.m. and wrote a statement. She informed Andrew and Tom that she would be delivering it later that morning and asked them to make the necessary arrangements.

That morning, I was not in the office because I was scheduled to meet with Bill Trudell for the first time. I didn't know him, but he had worked closely with Tom during the gas plant investigation, preparing staff being interviewed by the Legislative Committee. Anxiety had robbed me of any real sleep. I had been up as usual at five a.m., fretting. Just before eight a.m., an email arrived from Andrew sent to senior staff. It was the premier's statement, explaining her decision to stand by me. Near the end of this statement, there was this paragraph:

I have a terrific team of people who work for me. I rely on
their skill, their advice and their integrity every day. They
know how I work and they work with me because we share
a value system. When these entreaties from opposition
members were made, it was my staff, especially those who
have been political advisors for a long time, who were instantly adamant that we reject any such notion. They are
fine people with an explicit commitment to honest politics.
Pat Sorbara, particularly, is a seasoned professional and a
woman of integrity.

I put my head down on my table and I cried. I felt an immense
sense of relief and gratitude. It takes an exceptional person and politician to take a position different than what was clearly the easiest
road. Every member of the media in the room for the premier's press
conference assumed I would be made the scapegoat. When pressed,
she stated that if I was charged I would resign, but not before. She
did not believe I had done anything wrong, and it would be unfair to
make me leave my job. We had decided to fight.

Each day for three straight weeks, the NDP and PCS banded
together and dedicated every single question in question period to
Sudbury. Most of the questions demanded a resignation: mine, the
premier's, Glenn's or all three. The premier repeated what she had
said in her press conference: she did not believe I had done anything
wrong and I would not resign.

*Lesson: In very public moments, it can never be about staff or personal
ego. It is always about the politicians and the photo.*

Justin Trudeau made an appearance at Queen's Park on October 27,
2015, shortly after being elected prime minister. I had arranged for
a group of people to gather on the front steps of the main legislative building to welcome the new PM. I couldn't help but smile at
the people standing nearby to protest about another issue but who

stopped their chanting long enough to cheer for the new PM as he emerged from his vehicle. As the premier and PM moved toward the crowd, they walked by where I was standing. Given how crazy it had been around the Sudbury saga, I stepped aside and did not try to say hello.

But the PM spotted me, took a deliberate step behind the premier and crossed over to give me a hug. Although I could hear the applause of staff as they acknowledged the significance of the moment, it was background noise to my own feelings. I was overwhelmed with emotion. I was so happy for this man, and grateful that he had not let the controversy stop him from acknowledging me, regardless of what the media might think. In that moment, he was simply Justin to me.

We'd known each other from our short but intense work together in Ottawa, with him as a recently elected MP and me as the chief operating officer in the Office of the Leader of the Opposition. After I'd left Ottawa in July 2011, he and I and would occasionally chat on the phone (including a conversation we'd had about Glenn running for the Liberals). Justin knew I'd led the effort to ensure we followed through on the OLP's commitment of support to the federal Liberal Party. We had assigned needed resources to back up the ground effort in Ontario. He was grateful, and he'd taken that very public moment to say so. I told him how thrilled I was that he had won and sent him along to the waiting crowd.

Reporter Ashley Csanady of the Queen's Park gallery stated, "Even Wynne's embattled chief of staff Pat Sorbara—still under provincial investigation for her role in the Sudbury byelection scandal—gets a moment."

Although I was thrilled with the outcome of the federal election and desperately wanted to offer my congratulations to my friend Justin, I knew that my interaction with the PM might take away from what was a great news story. With that understanding firmly in my mind, I exercised the discipline to not draw any attention away from the PM and premier. The fact that Justin would bypass that reality to be kind to me, and to say thank you, meant a great deal to me and spoke to his understanding of all that the Ontario Liberal Party had done for him.

Lesson: The Centre exists and it's make-or-break.

I have witnessed the ugliness that can happen when those who work in the Centre develop an inward-looking siege mentality. It demands full buy-in to the theory that the Centre is always right and cannot be challenged. The fear becomes that if you challenge the authority of the Centre, you may be forced to leave it. That is essentially what happened to me in 2016, following the departure of Tom Teahen as chief of staff and consolidation of all power around Andrew Bevan.

By the end of the Wynne era, I believe we were seeing a Centre at its worst. Essentially, an "us versus the world" attitude took hold at its heart. If there are no guardians of the Centre who are motivated more by the health of the overall organization and less by power and control, then the Centre will fail at its job. And few would argue that it was anything other than a failure to do its job.

There are some who argue you never debate an issue in front of the premier or leader. It's my view that in positive working environments, respectful debate with the premier or leader is acceptable and even expected. It's why you are there and why you have a senior role. In some governments, power becomes concentrated in one or two people and it is with them that you are forced to have the debate. Essentially it means the premier's world becomes very narrow, listening to only a few senior advisors. There's nothing more dispiriting than engaging in a debate during a meeting and suddenly realizing the decision has already been made, based on a pre-meeting from which you were excluded. It means you either have to shut up or find another avenue to get your point of view in front of the premier.

Choosing a cabinet is a great example of this kind of debate. A highly stressful example of this for me was the cabinet shuffle in 2016. Generally, there are two or three discussions before the premier is left to make final decisions. If you are lucky enough to be in the room, you are extremely conscious of the impact of your input, on both the operation of the government and the individuals being considered. You are discussing the career futures of human beings who want nothing more than to be in cabinet, and you're acutely aware of how they will feel both if they are selected and if they aren't.

The issue was whether Glenn Thibeault would enter cabinet. The OPP investigation into the Sudbury saga was ongoing, but it had been made clear no charges were being considered against the premier or Glenn. In the first meeting, when Glenn's name came up, Premier Wynne shook her head and said Glenn could not go into the cabinet. I had assumed the opposite and said so. I argued he had earned his opportunity, and he would add considerable strength to the bench. Mostly I argued he should not continue to be punished by unfounded allegations that were still being investigated. If anyone had earned the right to go in, it was Glenn. It was clear there had been a pre-discussion and I was firmly shut down.

The next day, I sought an opportunity to speak one on one with the premier. Although nervous about the response I would get, I reminded her of what she had told Glenn in November 2014 when the party was recruiting him to run. A role in cabinet was not on the table at that point but she assured Glenn he'd have a fair opportunity at the next shuffle. I considered it unfortunate that the situation—one that was causing so much damage to my own reputation, despite being unfounded—was going to affect Glenn in this way. She stopped me mid-pitch and said, "Glenn's going in. He'll be terrific and I need him in cabinet." I was pretty excited when he was eventually given the significant but tough role of minister of energy.

Our cabinet rubber-stamped most decisions. From time to time, they would voice their concerns and demand greater consultation, but only on a few occasions did a plan get revisited. The rest of the caucus was left well out of the loop, to the point where caucus felt it had no control whatsoever about what its own government was doing. These MPPs were expected to ignore their reservations and support their government wholeheartedly. There was a growing uneasiness and uncertainty developing within the larger organization.

One of the most stressful examples was the changes to the fundraising rules and the *Elections Act*. Over many years, the party had perfected its highly successful fundraising machine known as the Ontario Liberal Fund. Led by the incredibly skilled Bobby Walman, it focused on corporate contributions. The government was taking a pounding on the issue known as "cash for access." The opposition and media developed a narrative over time that government decisions were directly related to how much corporations contributed (even though the opposition accepted money from the same corporations). Perception had become reality and several questionable decisions fuelled the fire.

We needed to follow the federal government and move away from corporate contributions. While some argued we should hold off until after the 2018 campaign, the consensus was to create new rules as quickly as possible. Attention turned to what changes should be made. We set up a committee of civil servants and political staff to study legislative changes. As the only experienced campaigner at the table, I considered it my job to argue the impact of the proposed changes on political parties—a key stakeholder—and campaigning.

I left government before the legislation was finished, having become chief executive officer of the Ontario Liberal Party, but prior to my departure, I was involved for several months as the legislative changes were drafted. It was an excellent illustration of the process designed to ensure changes met the needs of several competing elements, including the public and the chief electoral officer charged with administering the *Act*. In the end, that's not what happened.

The process was narrow and frustrating, and caucus was left completely out of it. Based on the timeline we set, it was determined there was no time to look at creative ideas or solutions (or even to consult, for that matter). Working closely with the director of policy, Gillian McEachern, we would get direction from Andrew Bevan every few days. A few times we directly briefed the premier, but usually

Andrew kept her up to date. There was no formal consultation on the bill as it was being drafted, and there were almost no informal discussions. I considered it a lost opportunity.

I urged Andrew to take the matter to caucus for input. He responded with a hard no, saying that the party and caucus were in a conflict of interest on the subject. That struck me as odd, as it was no different than any other situation where we consulted stakeholders impacted by upcoming legislation. I suggested we reach out to the NDP, the Conservatives and the Green Party for their general input on which rules made the most sense, but again I was told that political parties would have no say despite being directly impacted by the changes.

That left the chief electoral officer in a position to wield a lot of influence on the legislation. His views were driven by what was best for Elections Ontario and less about the voters. I often felt I was the only one arguing on behalf of the stakeholders, specifically the political parties and their candidates. The Premier's Office led the entire process, leaving the Attorney General's Office and outside stakeholders on the sidelines. And frankly, the legislation reflected it. When the draft legislation was finally discussed at caucus, MPPs reacted negatively to many of the proposed changes. They felt needed changes that impacted voters had been ignored. They made their views known but were told it was too late. We would proceed as planned.

I realized at the time that many caucus members were starting to feel unhappy about the leadership and its failure to listen to its own members. After I was charged and had left my roles, I learned of the wildest change of them all: elected officials could not attend their own fundraisers. It felt one step too far, as it crippled the ability of local MPPs to raise money. Andrew was the only one who seemed unable to recognize this, and yet he was the person who insisted the change be included.

It became clear to me that the Centre had failed badly by letting outside pressures dictate the outcome. A decision was made that the party would adopt the new rules immediately. It hurt us immensely, making it impossible to raise enough money to have a strong pre-writ campaign, as well as the funds needed to spend the limit allowed during the central campaign. Further, it left the Ontario Liberal Party in a precarious financial situation post-election. The most frustrating part of all was that the NDP and Conservatives, who had slammed the Liberals on the matter for months, carried on under the old rules and raised significant sums before the new rules took hold.

Lesson: If it's not working, take control of your own destiny and accept that change can be critical to your future success.

Life seemingly went back to normal (enough) as the investigations continued. And yet at some levels, I was under siege and it began to show. Some days seemed like nothing was happening, but other days we were at the barricades.

On the morning of September 24, 2015, Tom received news from Rick Bartolucci that Gerry had been charged criminally with one count of counselling an offence not committed, and one count of unlawfully influencing or negotiating appointments. It was a shock, as no one had been given a heads up. Bill managed to get a quick confirmation from the OPP that I was not being charged, but waiting for their response had been the longest sixteen minutes of my life. I remember the feeling of relief washing over me.

We don't really know what caused the OPP to charge Gerry and not me. My firm belief is that my excellent legal team did all they could to convince the OPP and the Crown that charges were not warranted, and there was insufficient evidence to prove the case in court. If there was a silver lining in Gerry being charged, it was that he got himself an outstanding defence lawyer, Michael Lacy. While working closely with my legal team, he made it clear his primary goal was to get the criminal charges against Gerry dropped.

On April 27, 2016, seven months after they were laid, the OPP announced the charges against Gerry were stayed. Instead of dropping them outright, as everyone expected, "stayed" meant they could be reintroduced at any time in the coming twelve months. No reason was given but it appeared political and punitive. Michael became an important person in my own defence. Once the charges were stayed against Gerry, he teamed up with my lawyers to push back, over the next six months, against the ongoing investigation under the *Election Act*.

January 2016 brought another development into my professional life, and not a good one. Tom Teahen, who had been the premier's chief of staff since Kathleen Wynne became premier, had resigned his position to return to the Workplace Safety and Insurance Board—this time as its president and CEO. Tom had shown me incredible personal and professional respect and support since we began working together. Andrew Bevan became chief of staff and kept his role as principal secretary. People were perplexed by the decision, as it meant all of the power became concentrated in one person rather than the normal set up of spreading it out among two or three very senior people. Not only did I see my own authority diminish but I soon found the tide turning against me.

Once Andrew took over as chief, I found myself excluded from meetings I would have attended when Tom was there. I was the chief operating officer and by definition, should have been in a number of meetings attended by senior staff where operational decisions were being made. I would hear about decisions after the fact and often Andrew would have assigned someone else to execute a decision before consulting with me. At one point I asked David Herle why Andrew disliked me. David's reply? "He likes you, he just thinks you are a bitch." That made me shake my head, thinking about all of the times people counted on the "bitch" to do the heavy lifting.

Eventually things came to a head. On June 10, 2016, Andrew advised me that I needed a reset. He said I was to take a vacation and come back refreshed and ready to undertake the upcoming by-election in Scarborough Rouge River. He went on to say that staff were complaining about how I treated them and some were even threatening to quit their jobs. I asked him for specifics. While admitting he'd never seen it, he stated he'd heard about it enough to believe it.

Andrew went on to say I wasn't getting my job done. He said the reason people went to him for answers was because they weren't hearing back from me. On top of that, I had been remiss in not yet appointing a campaign manager for the upcoming by-election in Scarborough Rouge River. In my entire working career of almost forty years, I had never had a meeting like that one. None of it made any sense to me. I became upset and confused by the certainty with which this information was presented.

At five p.m., after dropping this massive bombshell on that Friday afternoon, Andrew left me sobbing in his office. He had to pick up his son. Before he left, he said he was my friend and we'd work this out. I said I would be fine, I just needed time to sort out my thoughts. I pretty much cried for the rest of the day, and all day Saturday. By Sunday I started to get some perspective.

I was devastated by the suggestion that the entire senior staff did not want to work with me. My view was that a cabal had developed around Andrew, led by Rebecca Mackenzie, director of operations Chad Walsh and director of tour Mel Wright. They had begun to show a lot of resistance to my leadership, opposing a more disciplined and inclusive approach. My way of operating as a boss has been the same for a long time. My approach was to build a team of people who worked well together and treated one another with respect. But yes, those people understood I was in charge. There were established processes and protocols I expected to have met. I have never tolerated cabals.

I came to realize it wasn't my team. Andrew insisted on complete control and in that scenario, the coo role had no place. I thought a great deal about my options. I couldn't see a way to fix the situation and came to the decision I needed to leave the Premier's Office.

I asked for a meeting with Premier Wynne, Andrew as my boss at Queen's Park and David Herle as managing co-chair of the campaign to discuss how I could best serve the organization and the premier. It finally got scheduled on July 13, 2016, more than a month after my meeting with Andrew. I asked for the first ten minutes of the meeting to explain my side of things and then we could look at solutions. I had made notes to help me get through what I knew would be a very emotional conversation.

It was clear that overall, there had been a consolidation of authority around Andrew. I came to understand his management style was to manage directly. I explained I was okay with that, given it's also my style. But it meant direction went from the chief of staff directly the executive directors, leaving me out of the loop. I told Andrew that his cabal worked against the overall organization I had tried to institute, which resulted in me being unable to establish a meaningful role as a COO. I expressed my hurt because I thought they were friends who would talk to me if they had concerns about my behaviour. It was shocking to have been told I needed a reset with no heads up at all.

I put forward to the premier that I should shift to the party office, assuming the vacant role of chief executive officer of the Ontario Liberal Party in addition to the campaign director title I already held. There was no question serious focus needed to be turned to OLP and the campaign, even if it seemed earlier than usual that I'd leave the Premier's Office to start full-time campaign work. I felt my efforts were best put toward building up the OLP, both centrally and at the riding level. The base was seriously lacking, the foundation was showing cracks. My only caveat was that with this move, I would still be considered a member of senior staff.

The premier had stopped me halfway through my remarks, just after my suggestion that I move to OLP. She was visibly relieved, and admitted she'd been worried that my plan was to leave completely. She did not want that. When she and I talked afterward, she told me I had been very brave to say all of what I did in front of Andrew. Neither Andrew nor David said much in response to my remarks. There was agreement in the room that my plan made sense for all involved.

Although the conversation was in July, I did not make the move to the Party office until October 1, 2016. The Scarborough Rouge

River by-election was being called for September 1 and I took a few
weeks of vacation to be part of it. Liberals had held the seat since
1999, when it was first created. MPP Bas Balkissoon had left his role
unexpectedly and we, of course, wanted to keep the riding.

It became clear to me during that by-election that as a party, we
were in big trouble. Scarborough Rouge River is the most ethno-
culturally diverse riding in Ontario. We should have been able to
hold it. We ran a candidate from the Tamil community, but so did
the NDP. The PCs ran long-time city councillor Raymond Cho. We
lost by 2,387 votes, or 9.7 percent. We were neck and neck with the
NDP, allowing the PCs to come up the middle. They had the best-
known candidate and they used sex ed as a wedge issue, despite Patrick Brown stating publicly that he would not rescind the updated
sex ed curriculum that had been introduced that fall.

I threw myself into my new role as the chief executive officer of
the Ontario Liberal Party. I already knew most of the staff, but I
worked to build a team of people who understood our value as an
organization. My focus turned to two by-elections that were called
for November 17. Teams were set but once again, there was pushback
on my choice of campaign managers. My long-time assistant and
friend Mike Johnson moved to OLP with me, much to my great relief.

Mike had been an integral part of the cohesion between the party
and Queen's Park, bridging the work of staff through by-elections,
nomination meetings, AGMs and other party events where political
staff participated. His focus was riding redistribution, which had to
be done by the end of the year, and I was grateful to have him nearby
each day. His personal support made it possible for me to stay ahead of
everything I was feeling about the move and the ongoing investigation.

As all of this was happening, the OPP were still investigating. Despite the intense efforts by our lawyers to convince the OPP not to
lay charges under the *Election Act*, they admitted they weren't getting very far. The OPP and Crown thwarted all attempts to convince
them that the evidence did not support a reasonable prospect of conviction. In the end, we got word the charges would proceed. It was

beyond anyone's understanding what evidence the Crown and OPP had that convinced them they could win in court. It turned out that all they felt they needed was a storyline they'd convinced themselves would hang together.

Along with the suggestion that I had bribed Andrew to leave the nomination race, I was also charged with bribing Glenn to enter the race. Somehow the OPP came to believe I had lured Glenn to leave his MP role, despite having to take a sizeable pay cut with no guarantee of winning the by-election and being told he would not be in cabinet. What he'd get in exchange was not even for him: it was alleged I had promised "jobs" to Brian Band and Darrell Marsh, two of the men who worked in Glenn's MP constituency office. Those "jobs" were in fact honorariums to acknowledge their work on the campaign and to provide a little bit of income replacement, given they had left their full-time positions. Brian received $2,600 and Darrell received $2,000. With one month under my belt in the new CEO role, the OPP advised us on October 31, 2016 that charges would be laid the next day.

Lesson: While you should always hope for the best, it's imperative to be ready for the worst.

It was an incredibly tough few days as I managed through the practical realities of being charged. The premier had always said if I was charged, I would resign. The time had come. My resignation letter read as follows:

> As you are aware, today there was a decision that I will be charged with a provincial offence under the *Election Act.* Despite the fact that I was earlier cleared of any criminal wrongdoing, as I indicated to you some time ago, I will be resigning from my position as CEO of the Ontario Liberal Party as well as Campaign Director of the Ontario Liberal Party.

I continue to believe, with my whole heart, as I have from the beginning, that any charge against me will not succeed. I am shocked by any suggestion that I have done anything wrong. I will defend myself against these allegations to the best of my ability and with the tremendous support that surrounds me.

I have served my entire career with integrity and a deep respect for the law. This is very hard for me. During the time that I am dealing with these matters, I do not want in any way for our Party to be tarnished during the process.

It is my hope that as soon as possible I will be able to serve the community and contribute again.

My resignation letter was the only public statement I would make until the press conference the day the judge threw out the charges. As the debate and accusations raged on in the media, in the legislature and in the campaign offices, I had no way to respond to the public comments being made about the circumstances that led to the charges.

Ignoring the appeal from my lawyers that they now leave the matter to the courts, the media reached their own conclusions, stoked by the relentless questions in the legislature. The opposition critics put their own spin on every detail they could uncover. There was no regard to due process or fairness. I was guilty in the legislature and the media before I had any opportunity to defend myself. We could only stay quiet and await the trial. It was frustrating and it hurt. It harmed my reputation, personally and professionally.

For me, it was heart-wrenching and hard to accept. Within twenty-four hours I had lost two jobs, but what made things worse was that without any discussion it was decided my leave of absence from the government would be cancelled and I would be formally terminated. That action ended all ties to the government and the party. It was a lot to take. I had always understood that my leave of absence from government would remain intact, allowing me to continue to pay into the pension plan and receive benefits. Moreover, it meant I could easily transition back to work when the time came. I suddenly found myself at sixty years old with no job and no benefits.

Compensation-wise, the party and Kathleen Wynne were beyond fair. My salary was paid throughout the waiting period and the trial and my legal fees were covered. It created a huge financial burden for the OLP and I will be forever grateful to them for that support. They went out of their way to acknowledge all I had contributed to the party and that I had done nothing wrong. Over the next few days I got hundreds of supportive messages from friends, family and Liberal staffers. They worried about my well-being, and they worried about what would happen with the campaign without me there. One of the few shining moments was when I saw David Herle's Facebook post that read, over a photo of the two of us, "Pat will be there when we win in 2018." That was certainly the plan.

On November 2, I met with Bill in the lobby of the Shangri-La Hotel to talk about next steps. He told me he would not be the lawyer who would take my case to court, as he needed to continue overall coordination of the many legal teams involved. I burst into tears, overcome at yet another loss. He assured me that Erin Dann, who had worked this case from the beginning, would be there to the end. He then told me he'd lined up a lawyer to take his place: the indomitable Brian Greenspan. Feeling a surge of hope, I stopped crying as suddenly as I started, looked at him and said, "Bill, you could have led with that." We laughed and talked about next steps.

My first meeting with Brian took place on November 5 at his office. Bill and Erin were both there. Despite the comfort of their presence, I was intimidated by the thought of meeting Brian, one of the top ten defence lawyers in the country. He put me immediately at ease, telling me about growing up in Niagara Falls, being a young Liberal and his admiration for his political hero, Liberal MP Judy LaMarsh, the second woman to serve as a federal cabinet minister.

I pressed the lawyers about how quickly we could get to trial, knowing that was my only route back to work. With the election only eighteen months away, I needed to be back at the helm as quickly as possible. Their response was that it was going to take some time. I was now just another person waiting for trial and I was hardly a priority in the context of the justice system. The trial would take place in Sudbury and court time would be assigned when it was available for a trial that would need several days to complete. A judge had yet to be assigned to the case but when someone was named, schedules would have to be coordinated.

In fact, the trial dates were not set until February 3, 2017, and on the same day, Erin emailed to let me know Judge Howard Borenstein was assigned as the trial judge. Erin and Brian agreed Judge Borenstein would not be influenced by the politics surrounding the case; he'd make his judgement based on the evidence. We spent the next months preparing for trial. I spent hundreds of hours going through the disclosure materials. I knew the lawyers would do their work, but I felt I had to do my part.

I looked for the nuggets, the small stuff that might be a signal as to how the OPP were approaching the case. I read each interview transcript, some several times. I reviewed the emails over and over. I found it mildly amusing that I had provided the OPP almost every email they used as evidence. I reviewed a large percentage of the police notes, even though Erin assured me they would have no relevance in the courtroom. It was the evidence that mattered, not what the police thought. The entire exercise became an opportunity to learn. And learn I did—much of it related to how the OPP had long pre-judged the case. It was striking to me that over and over the OPP seemed to push back any theory or evidence put forward by the defence. They seemed determined to charge.

Lesson: Teaching someone on the outside about the inner workings of politics is like trying to teach them a new language.

I had spent a lot of time over the months helping the lawyers understand how it worked in political backrooms. Like most of the general public, they had no real idea of how partisan politics worked and the culture in which we operated. For example, with the help of several people, we had produced a binder full of examples of similar nomination situations where an individual was asked, or opted, to step aside for a preferential or star candidate. It was a long list of examples of internal party contests (nominations or leaderships) in which a candidate for nomination, and in some cases a sitting elected official, stepped aside in favour of another candidate (typically a candidate preferred by the Centre). These included the following:

- Steve Ryan for Doug Holyday (Etobicoke Lakeshore, 2013 byelection)
- Jean Augustine for Michael Ignatieff (Etobicoke Lakeshore, 2006 federal election)
- Martha Hall Findlay for Belinda Stronach (Newmarket, 2006 federal election)
- Rob Oliphant for Bob Rae (Toronto Centre, 2007 federal by-election)
- Abdul Ingar and Deborah Coyne for Rob Oliphant (Don Valley West, 2008 federal election)
- Sachin Aggarwal for Glenn Murray (Toronto Centre, 2010 provincial by-election)
- Ken Chan for Arnold Chan (Scarborough – Agincourt, 2013 federal by-election)
- Christine Tabbert for Adam Vaughan (Trinity Spadina, 2014 federal by-election)
- Barj Dhahan for Harjit Singh Sajjan (Vancouver South, 2015 federal election)

During the investigation, Garfield Dunlop had resigned as MPP to allow Patrick Brown to gain the seat of Simcoe North. It caused a by-election which Patrick won handily. Although he denied it at the beginning, it was well known locally that Dunlop had been given a job as an advisor to the leader of the opposition. How he was paid (through the PC Party, it eventually came out in the media) did not make a difference. Dunlop had stepped aside for the leader of his party and was given a job in return. Another high-profile situation had happened in early 2009, when Laurie Scott resigned to allow newly elected leader John Tory to gain a seat in the legislature. Scott immediately went to work with the Ontario PC Party. These examples helped the lawyers understand how candidate recruitment worked and in particular, the balance between finding the best possible candidates and keeping the process as open as possible.

It took some time to explain why candidates prefer an acclamation over an appointment. Contested nominations are incredibly tough and are generally avoided by people who haven't come through the ranks. Beyond that, candidates being recruited because of their profile or special interest prefer it to look like the opposition stepped aside in support as opposed to being pushed aside to clear the way. It's just human nature to want to avoid starting your campaign with people unhappy with you.

All parties follow the rules of procedure outlined in their constitutions and in most the leader has some prerogative to appoint; in the Ontario PC Party, the leader had an unfettered right to appoint all candidates. In the public domain, where nomination meetings are wrongly equated with general elections, it's seen as inherently unfair and undemocratic to not have an open nomination. To avoid a negative reaction, candidates prefer that someone magically handle things behind the scenes.

I explained to the lawyers why the role of Gerry Lougheed was critical in the political environment. People like Gerry are often called "kingmakers," and it was not an unfair assessment. They generally have run the local party for a long time and riding-level Liberals listen to them. To the OLP, Gerry was critical to success both locally and centrally. He made things happen in the Sudbury area. For years Gerry worked closely with Rick Bartolucci and made sure he had enough money to win election after election. Gerry was an old-style operator and Rick was an old-style politician.

On my call with Andrew I made the statement that Premier Wynne was "desperate" to get the riding, which I immediately qualified as "desperate in a good way." It was the perfect example of interpreting a phrase to reflect how you choose to see the situation. I used the word to highlight that winning back Sudbury was a key priority from a political perspective. Yet the opposition and the OPP pushed the theory that my comment meant we would bribe Andrew, out of desperation. It was evident the OPP would not be giving me the benefit of the doubt on anything. My words were challenged and my motivation rejected.

The unexpected charge that I had bribed Glenn to leave his MP role to run was perplexing to everyone. After the charge was announced, the media reacted strongly, suggesting that if I had bribed Glenn, it didn't make sense that he had not been charged with accepting the bribe. On November 21, 2016, at the first pre-trial conference in Sudbury, Crown prosecutor Vern Brewer made the comment that the section of *Act* in play made it an offence to offer but not necessarily receive a bribe. He stated, "The allegation in respect to that count relates to our allegation that Mr. Thibeault sought certain benefits, offers or jobs or employment as part of his conditions to run as MPP."

All hell broke loose. Glenn's lawyer, Ian Smith, responded immediately, calling Brewer's comments factually incorrect and "supremely frustrating." Smith wrote in a statement, "The Crown has chosen to sully Mr. Thibeault's reputation without ever naming him as the target of its investigations, without ever charging him and, most importantly, knowing that he will have no trial where he could mount a proper defence."

The political nature of the Crown's comments stunned everyone. The opposition ran with it and called for Glenn to resign from cabinet. At the time, the general assumption was that the offer must have been a cabinet position. People were quite surprised to learn much later that, in fact, it referenced stipends paid to two trusted staff members for their work on the campaign. Glenn was upset and hurt but was clear he would not be resigning. True to form, he was more concerned about his family and kids, stating to the media through tears, "To have your name slandered all over the place and your family has to deal with that? That's extremely difficult."

While Brewer attempted to backpedal by saying Glenn was not under investigation, the damage had been done. I believe the Crown's actions were deliberate and meant to undermine Glenn as a witness. After a month of legal back and forth, including a threatened lawsuit against Brewer, the Public Prosecution Service of Canada and the Attorney General of Canada, the PPSC finally retracted the statement.

During the lead-up to the trial, David Herle and I would meet regularly at the Thompson Diner, near his home. At our last breakfast before I headed to Sudbury, David told me everything was riding on the outcome of the trial, which of course included that I needed to return and run the campaign. But for the first time, he added an element that I had not considered: his view was that if I was found guilty, Premier Wynne would have to resign. With everything that had happened, she was too closely aligned to the case and to me. If I was guilty, she was guilty. I left there slightly freaked out, but more motivated than ever to win the case.

During the same months we prepared for trial, I worked to stay in touch with what was happening at the party and for election readiness. Chad Walsh, whom I had worked with since 2008 in both Ottawa and Toronto, had been appointed interim campaign director—on my recommendation. It was originally agreed that David, Chad and I would meet regularly to go through the critical path and look to see how I could keep up to date and to provide input where it would helpful. The first few meetings did not go well, and I sensed resistance from Chad.

Perhaps I should have recognized the early warning signs. David felt perhaps I was pushing too hard and needed to step back and let Chad find his feet. That summer, Chad was quietly moved from interim campaign director to campaign director. I decided not to overreact because I wanted what was best for the campaign. Despite emails, outreach, commitments and promises, I was never sent a critical path to review. I actually don't know of anyone who saw it. I think ultimately Chad decided it wasn't needed and no one held him accountable.

CHAPTER 10

The Courage of Your Convictions
Will Carry You Through

"When you get into a tight place and everything goes against you,
till it seems as though you could not hang on a minute longer,
never give up then, for that is just the place and the time that the
tide will turn."
– Harriet Beecher Stowe

The first day of trial, September 7, was my sixty-first birthday.
I was ready but it was still felt like somehow I'd wake up
and the nightmare would be over. I had been strictly counselled
on courtroom behaviour. It was a good thing given that I am
known to react visibly. There was to be no unusual emotion in the
courtroom. I was to act as neutral as possible. I was not to communicate with the judge in any way. There was to be no talking
or whispering.

We had a system where if I needed to make a point urgently, I
was to write it on a Post-it Note and give it to Erin. If she decided
it was critical, she would pass it onto Brian. Otherwise we'd hold it
for discussion at the break. I managed my emotion by writing in the
notebook I kept in front of me at all times. Lots and lots of notes.
Sometimes I had questions but mostly I wrote to keep calm and focused. Sometimes the language got so legalistic and complicated that
I had to stop writing and just listen.

In the middle of the book I had a few pages of photos I would look at when I needed to be distracted from what was going on in the courtroom. They were photos of my great-nieces, Lucy, Eloise, Sophie and Juliette; the sons of my friends Jackie and Phil Playfair, Graeme and Iain; my dog Nellie; and the kids and pets of other friends and family. When I looked at them, I'd bring myself back to balance and try to remember what really mattered in life. I added in the one David had put on Facebook, saying I'd be back when we won in 2018. That one gave me hope. It was also comforting to know that in a way, I was indirectly tethered back to the Liberal family through staff person Swarj Mann, who was in the courtroom every day taking notes and reporting back to the Liberal Caucus.

I had teased the lawyers about what appeared to me to be a very short court day. The plan was to start at 10 a.m., take a fifteen-minute break at eleven thirty a.m., have lunch at one p.m., return at 2:15 p.m., and take a second break in the afternoon as needed. I joked that in politics, that kind of day would be a luxury. But once we got underway, I quickly understood the schedule. Every minute felt intense and it required immense concentration to listen and follow the questions and dialogue between the judge and the lawyers. I realized how important it was to give the judge time to absorb what he was learning, to check his notes, to form his thoughts. At the end of the first day, I sheepishly retracted my uninformed opinion.

I was warned to expect the first two days to heavily favour the prosecution, as they would have control of the narrative during the opening and while Andrew was on the stand. The defence would not get a word in until it was time to cross-examine Andrew. But that's not what happened. On that very first morning, the defense was able to take control of the debate when the court played a second recorded conversation between me and Andrew. Andrew's testimony began that first day and lasted into the next. It was surreal sitting there hearing my voice when they played the two conversations I'd had with Andrew about his interest in being a candidate in the by-election. I listened to myself say, "You are the past candidate, not the current candidate, yet."

In some ways, Andrew was no different than any other person I've known who wanted to be a candidate. Unhappy it wasn't going to happen, he turned our efforts to treat him fairly and openly into something personal. Anyone who has worked within a political party knew it. No true partisan would hurt the party the way Andrew did, no matter how disappointed they were by the decision.

Lesson: There are so many different personalities in politics, and your approach to each individual situation could never be "one size fits all." You have to learn to anticipate the wild card.

I must admit how surprised I was when I first heard the tape of the conversation between Gerry and Andrew. I was stunned by his suggestion to Andrew that the premier wanted to present options to him in terms of appointments or jobs, and that Andrew should ask himself, "What's in it for me?" Gerry is what I call a "cowboy," sometimes acting with considerable swagger. (It's usually reserved for staff and is a person who means well, knows the ground, is comfortable in their skin but generally can't follow protocols.) The OPP suggested that Gerry's role in the party and stature in the community put undue pressure on Andrew. For his part, Gerry felt they were friends, allowing him to talk about the situation in a friendly way.

What I had told the OPP struck me again in court as I listened to the tape. I believed Gerry had projected onto Andrew how he would have wanted things to work. In some ways, Gerry came from old-style politics, always looking for opportunities. For every demand, there was a reward and for a long time he and Rick had worked together on appointments for the area. I knew Gerry was giving Andrew advice, not trying to bribe him. But had I been aware of the exact language Gerry had used, I would never have put the premier on the phone with Andrew. We had never discussed that approach and it never would have happened.

The premier and I had talked about whether we would have done it any differently. We concluded we would not have. Telling Andrew about the decision that Glenn would be the candidate was the respectful and fair thing to do. But practically, if I'd known how it all would end, I expect I would have put fairness a little lower on the list, at least where Andrew was concerned.

As the trial got underway, those following along quickly recognized the terrible job being done by the OPP and the Crown. They were unprepared, they rambled and stumbled, their presentation was confusing and their case incoherent. It only took a few days for the media to start pointing out the holes in their case.

The Crown regularly referred to the need for "secrecy," suggesting that because it was hidden, it had to be wrong. It was instead about Glenn's ask that his family be given the opportunity to celebrate Christmas before everything went wild.

At some point, the Crown advanced a theory that Andrew's December 15 press conference, at which he stated he was bribed and withdrew his interest in running for the Liberals, was a "Hail Mary pass." He hoped his response would pressure the premier into holding a contested nomination meeting. But he had blown the situation wide open and made serious accusations. It made no sense to run the risk of further discussion.

Michael began his cross-examination in the last half hour of the first day. I wondered why he'd pushed to get going with so little time left. It was explained to me afterward that once the cross-examination was underway, the Crown could no longer interface with the witness. In order to be sure Andrew had no further prep with the Crown, it was important to start the cross.

On day one, Michael had brought home two critical points: Andrew admitted he knew he was not a candidate, only that he had declared an interest in running for the nomination. And that no one on trial influenced his decision to run as an independent. Michael gave Andrew every opportunity during the cross-examination to say bluntly that he felt bribed; that in return for stepping down as a candidate, there would be something of value awarded to him. Except Andrew never did say it because given the full context, it could not be true.

Michael pointed out that during the November 12, 2015, interview—nearly a year after the taped conversations—Detective Sergeant Evans asked Andrew, "I think I'd just like to ask you this question right out. In any of the conversations you had with the three individuals I've just identified, were you of the opinion that you were being offered some reward benefit for withdrawing your intention to be a nominee for the Liberal party?" Andrew had replied, "Um, yes, I would say that, you know, with an opportunity to be within the party. I had no interest in finding out if these were paid positions, non-paid positions, nothing was specifically offered, no specific job, but my understanding and impression of those conversations was there was something, you know, as again I said, as a consolation prize is—quote, unquote—for, you know, endorsing and moving aside."

Andrew was clear under cross-examination that his impression from the conversations was that he was being offered an opportunity within the party. And that no one had directly offered an appointment in the government. I admit that in those moments I felt a great sense of pride in, and satisfaction on behalf of, the defence counsel. I had worked hard to teach them about the political process and how things are done in the backroom. To hear them effortlessly, accurately and sensibly explain the process in a way that was impactful for the room and the judge made me feel my efforts had paid off.

Andrew could never be accused of being a strong witness for the prosecution. It was clear he was uncomfortable the entire time he was on the stand, even unhappy to be there. From time to time he even got a little hostile when the Crown pushed him for a certain answer. Everyone thought it odd the Crown did not re-examine Andrew after the defence completed the cross-examination. I think they realized Andrew was not helping their case.

It's important to remember that Andrew did not initiate the complaints that eventually led to the charges. I believe he was upset and angry. He released the tapes as a form of revenge and a way to help his run in the by-election. But did he intend to put Gerry, Glenn and the premier through what followed? I doubt it very much.

NDP MPP Gilles Bisson, who did initiate the complaint to Elections Ontario, showed up in the courtroom on the second day of trial. Seemingly unhappy about the media reports from the first day, it appeared his plan was to try to insert himself into the stories to change the narrative. When Gilles was back again at the start of the third day, the media began to ask him why he was sitting in a courtroom in Sudbury rather than doing his job as House leader for the NDP.

Questions about the case were still being asked in the legislature, even though the trial was underway. It was shocking to see the both the NDP and the Tories ask questions about the testimony that had been given the day before in court, making it clear that due process for me and Gerry was quite secondary to their need to score political points. Within a few days—I'm sure based on a complaint from Yasir Naqvi, the government House leader—Speaker Dave Levac finally ruled questions about Sudbury out of order, after allowing them for two years.

Over the fall, the PCs began running pre-writ ads. David Herle had told me to prepare for the PCs to use my name in an ad, and they did. You hear Patrick Brown say, "their most senior campaign operator is facing bribery charges" while in the background the words read, "Liberal Pat Sorbara charged with bribing Glenn Thibeault to defect from the NDP," sourcing a CBC News–Sudbury story.

Lesson: As the saying goes, "the devil is in the details." In politics, it's a constant battle between how to get your message across quickly and the value of context.

The day after the start of the trial, the headline of the *Toronto Star* article by Rob Ferguson was, "Olivier tells Sudbury by-election trial he's not sure he was offered paid jobs to step aside." It made you wonder—if he wasn't a candidate and he did not feel bribed, why were we there? As early as September 11, media were starting to question the purpose of the trial and the basis for the charges. An editorial in the *Chronicle Journal* (the newspaper of northwest Ontario) stated,

"Meanwhile, the finer points of the *Election Act* notwithstanding, it seems difficult to conclude that Pat Sorbara, Wynne's former chief of staff, and Sudbury Liberal fundraiser Gerry Lougheed, did anything that was particularly heinous or unusual in the rough-and-tumble world of provincial politics, based on what has been heard at the trial so far."

The third day of the trial, September 11, started with Simon Tunstall who was executive director of OLP during the by-election. Much focus was put on an assessment he sent to me shortly after Cimino's resignation, and before he was aware we'd recruited Glenn to run. He told the court, "Well, I actually believed we were gonna lose... governing parties just don't pick up seats in by-elections." Simon admitted during the cross-examination by Michael that he did not believe a candidate like Glenn existed. He agreed that getting Glenn to run and winning with him was "quite the accomplishment."

Simon's comments spoke to why, when given the opportunity to win back Sudbury, we searched for the strongest candidate we could find. I found it odd that the Crown brought forward witness after witness who did not support their theories. It was during Simon's testimony that issues associated with the second charge against me were introduced for the first time, leading to a comical moment.

Brian asked Simon about my use of the word "urgent" in the subject line of the email I'd sent to him, relating to the income replacement payments I authorized for the individuals who had previously worked with Glenn in his constituency office, Brian Band and Darrell Marsh. Simon apologized before going on to say that I used the word "urgent" and the "high importance" symbol more than anyone he knew, by a significant margin. I glanced up, having been warned it was coming, and made eye contact with a sheepish Simon, while everyone chuckled.

More importantly, Simon made it clear that income replacement was common. It was not unusual to pay someone to work on a campaign or that volunteers became paid staff in order to allow them to dedicate more time.

September 13 was perhaps the most fascinating day of the trial for me because it was the day Domenic Giroux testified. His testimony, based on a text he'd sent me while we worked to recruit Glenn to run, had the potential to do the most damage. It was strange to watch Domenic try to act as if he was not fully involved in the push to get Glenn to run as a Liberal. It was from Domenic that we learned of Glenn's interest and he had inserted himself into the process right from the start.

I was uncomfortable with Domenic's involvement because as the president of Laurentian University, he was someone who should be neutral in his role. I've never been big on the clandestine stuff, where someone appeared neutral to the outside world but was happy to play politics behind the scenes. It was a lesson Domenic learned the hard way.

Domenic told the court that he was aware eighteen months before the by-election that Glenn was thinking about leaving federal politics. And that if he decided to run provincially, it would not be with the NDP party because he did not have a good relationship with the local association, but mostly because he had become very impressed with Kathleen Wynne.

In the midst of the recruitment process, I became concerned about the advice Domenic was giving to Glenn. The source of my concern was a text Domenic sent to me outlining a conversation he'd had with Glenn, which stated:

> The premier said he could only get in cabinet after a process and that the shuffle at a date to be determined. With your comment I personally would not do it without a clear commitment to a meaningful role in cabinet otherwise why bother? And too he has nothing if he loses this bye-lection so we'll ask you if he could get a commitment for an alternative role for a while if he isn't successful, keeping in mind that the turnout in a byelection is low, even more so in winter, which means anything can happen. He would

insist on a short open nomination and would only do if Andrew Olivier pulls back.

It was bizarre and it was not going to help our cause. Of particular
concern was Domenic telling Glenn he needed to ask for a cabinet
position and should he not win, a job. When I received the text, I sat
in my office having a minor panic attack about Domenic's bad advice.
I was uncertain how much influence Domenic had over Glenn. The
suggestion that Glenn would run only if Andrew withdrew, I knew
not to be true. But the Crown would later attempt to use it to advance a theory around what motivated our discussions with Andrew.

Domenic presented the issues as concerns Glenn raised with him,
but they were inconsistent with our discussions with Glenn, and flew
in the face of the discussion between Premier Wynne and Glenn just
a few days before. I called the premier. She agreed with my concerns
and suggested I involve Tom Teahen, who had worked closely with
Domenic at the Ministry of Education. I sent Tom an email with
Domenic's texts copied into them, making several points:

- this is old-style politics; the premier does not work this way
- you know the premier outlined her practice and process to
  Glenn and he indicated he was fine with it
- we need him to help us get Glenn to a decision to run without
  the commitment outlined in Dominic's texts; in terms of why
  bother, Glenn told the premier he wants to make a difference
- if he runs and wins he will be able to do just that and the rest
  will take care of itself
- we cannot have this many voices in Glenn's head, particularly
  if they conflict with what the premier has discussed with
  Glenn.

Tom and I talked and then he called Domenic. Other than Tom
confirming he'd reached Domenic, I did not hear much more about it
until Domenic was on the witness stand. Domenic's testimony helped

lay the groundwork that the only commitment made to Glenn to get him to run was a fully funded, professionally run campaign. The issue assumed to be most important to Glenn, an appointment to cabinet, had been taken off the table by the premier on November 30.

Domenic explained he was contacted by Tom. What I did not know until his testimony was that the call had been formal and stern. Tom stated in no uncertain terms there would be nothing given to Glenn in exchange for his decision to run and in particular, there would be no cabinet position. After that, Domenic made the decision to withdraw from any further discussions with Glenn or with me. And yet Domenic's text became central to many of the ensuing arguments.

The highly anticipated day of Premier Wynne's testimony dawned: September 13, 2017, day five of the trial, and she was scheduled to testify at nine a.m.

Michael joined us at the pre-meeting but said he needed to leave early to do a bit more prep. Erin headed out with him but a few seconds later, she was back. Michael had told her to wait and walk in with me and Brian. Her senior role in the case needed to be recognized, which meant being with me during the high-profile moments. It spoke to the importance of giving a woman credit, which, regardless of the profession, is something I've strived for my entire career.

It was the largest media day of the trial. As we went into court, I walked by the journalists lined up in the hallway. It could have a cabinet day at Queen's Park. I greeted them by name, feeling strangely happy to see the faces of people I knew, forgetting for a moment why we were there. I appreciated the kind greetings and warm smiles I received in response.

The premier took the stand promptly at nine a.m. She stood through the entire four hours of her testimony with only a single break. When Brewer asked the premier about her relationship with me and our history together, I was touched by her response: "I have known of Ms. Sorbara and her excellent reputation for many, many years." I looked down and wrote a note in my book to cover my emotion. I made direct eye contact with her only once. In that brief moment we acknowledged our friendship and affection and it brought me close to tears again. I know she felt the same sadness that I did in having to see each other in this way—me as a defendant and her as a witness at my trial. It was heart-wrenching.

While she was taking a respectful position in all her answers, I could see her wondering what the Crown's line of questioning was all about. At times I saw a bit of exasperation, but she covered it quickly. The Crown insisted on constantly making reference to an "open, democratic nomination process" when it had been clearly established that the OLP constitution dictated the rules for the nomination of candidates. The premier did not take the bait.

Brewer asked Premier Wynne, "Did you want to win the seat back?" Her response, "One always wants to win elections," said with a chuckle, caused a ripple of laughter through the courtroom. But it spoke to the key issue of why we were in the room. There was an awkward moment when Brewer referred the premier to a tab in the exhibit book. It became clear that the binder given to her did not match with the binder the judge was using. Controlling his annoyance, the judge instructed the Crown to resolve the issue at the break. The most critical witness in the trial and the premier of the province was testifying in front of the entire Queen's Park press gallery; that moment demonstrated the Crown's lack of attention to detail. As an organizer, I was appalled.

Premier Wynne was unequivocal that on their call on December 11, she had told Andrew that if she needed to, she would appoint Glenn. She was equally clear that any discussion around what Andrew might be interested in doing involved a process; it was not an automatic outcome. She explained how difficult and circular the conversation had become but she was reluctant to force the issue since Andrew had only gotten the news of Glenn's candidacy a few hours prior to their call.

Brewer asked the question, "Why not just appoint Glenn and move on?" The premier explained we were likely headed in that direction, but we wanted to try to bring Andrew around. As well, we were trying to find a way to hold Glenn's announcement until after Christmas.

The premier had waived parliamentary privilege, voluntarily participating in investigations, witness prep and testifying. She could have hidden behind her position but opted to be transparent and open. The premier was given the opportunity to clarify what we were thinking around how to let Andrew know of the circumstances. I felt her answer was critically important. She stated that regardless of the words Gerry used and the approach he took, she had clarified the entire situation with Andrew just a few hours later.

I felt very good in that moment because I had long been upset that the premier's conversation with Andrew had not been taped. I made the argument over and over that by the time I made my call to Andrew, he knew the lay of the land, directly from the leader.

During cross-examination, Brian gave the premier the opportunity to be clear why Glenn was such an attractive candidate to us and why she was confident others would see it the same way. She explained the government majority was not huge, the riding should never have been lost, and to her, every riding mattered. Winning the by-election meant it would be easier to hold Sudbury in the next general campaign. And to politicians, an acclamation is preferable to an appointment.

And finally, the key question of the trial was asked in a direct manner. What did we want in return for Andrew agreeing to support Glenn? The premier explained we wanted Andrew to stay involved but there was no quid pro quo for stepping aside. She wanted him to learn more and bring his perspective to the riding and the party. After the re-examination finished, we broke for lunch. I was relieved it was finally over for the premier.

Lesson: Some people don't like the saying, "It's just politics" but sometimes it couldn't be more true. You need a thick skin to differentiate between what's about you and what's about the partisan fight.

We headed over to the Motley Kitchen for lunch, which was our usual practice. But on this day, I came face to face with Jeff Ballingal, the former Harper staffer who runs the mean-spirited and nasty "Ontario Proud" and "Canada Proud" social media sites. I had been approached by media several times over the months but nothing so terrible as being yelled at by a man who entered my personal space with intent to demean and diminish, asking me, "Who is paying your legal bills?" "When did you last speak to Kathleen Wynne?" and "Aren't you ashamed of yourself?"

It took me a few seconds to get through the shock, at which moment I used my standing line, which was to refer to all questions to my lawyers. But Jeff demanded an answer, saying they were simple questions. As I continued to the restaurant, he continued to yell. I glanced back at the usual group of media standing together a few feet away and could see them shaking their heads as Jeff carried on.

Lesson: There is no substitute for doing your homework. Even if you think you're prepared, rerun every possible scenario.

September 14 was a very different day and we were back to the drudgery of witnesses who added little to the narrative, at least for the Crown. Darrell Marsh and Brian Band, the two individuals who worked in Glenn's constituency office when he was the NDP MP, were each called to the stand. There was a comical moment when Crown prosecutor David McKercher asked Darrell if he knew Patricia Sorbara. When Darrell indicated he knew me, McKercher said, "And who is she?" Darrell nodded toward me and responded, "She'd be the lady sitting over there," replicating the dramatic scene in more than one movie when the witness points to the defendant. Over the laughter, McKercher quickly clarified his question was about my role.

The next witness was Brian Band. In the midst of his testimony, we beheld perhaps the strangest moment of the trial. Reading from his list of questions, which were identical to the questions he had asked Darrell, McKercher asked Brian, "Who is Brian Band?" The courtroom reacted with confusion, as Brian responded with, "I beg your pardon?" McKercher asked again, "Who is Brian Band"? In what felt like a very existential moment, Brian responded, "This is me. I am, I am Brian Band." Simultaneously several people including defence counsel shouted out, "He's Brian Band."

On September 16, Mike Crawley and Erik White of the CBC put out an article entitled, "Four key things we've learned in the Sudbury by-election bribery trial." We were twelve witnesses in and we'd learned the following:

1. Olivier was not in line to be the candidate.
2. Olivier got no specific job offers—this was based on Olivier's direct testimony saying that we didn't get into details and that he "wasn't sure" I was talking to him about a paid job.
3. Thibeault decided to become a candidate before his staff got jobs.
4. The jobs for Thibeault's staff lasted a few weeks and paid little.

Day nine of the trial, September 19, Glenn testified. He was the last witness to be called by the Crown and the second most critical person to be called to the stand. During Glenn's testimony, the Crown once again headed down the road of conjecture.

During the cross-examination, Brian clarified with Glenn the "commitments" made by the premier: a well-organized, professionally run and fully funded campaign, that Sudbury mattered and that the Party was committed to winning back the riding. Glenn told the court the key things he and the premier discussed that day included their shared belief in the need for a progressive agenda; his personal interest in issues that are provincial; and that the legislature not sitting on Fridays would give him more time in the riding and with his family but allow him to remain in public service. The premier was clear Glenn would not have to fight for the nomination. Glenn agreed that he knew, leaving the meeting, he'd be the candidate if he wanted it.

Glenn was firm he had not made a demand for a role in cabinet and he did not ask for a job should he lose the election.

Glenn stated on the stand that he'd not had conversations with Brian and Darrell about getting paid, nor were they expecting it. He was aware by then that they were likely going to join him, but they had not yet talked about income replacement.

Among the strangest theories the Crown advanced was that my decision to bribe Andrew was based on my belief that without his support, Glenn might back out of the agreement to be our candidate. It seemed this late-breaking OPP hypothesis undoubtedly came from the text message sent by Domenic. No one had asked me about it, and no one had asked Glenn if Andrew's support was a deal-breaker. They had it so wrong. It seemed to me at that point, they were throwing spaghetti at the wall, in the hope something would stick.

During the re-examination by Crown prosecutor Rick Visca, clearly on the ropes, things got pretty intense. Glenn's testimony was that, while he talked about elements like income replacement for himself and for his staff, none of it was quid pro quo. Everything being discussed was in the context of a professionally run campaign. He clarified that many of his questions were in relation to how the Liberal Party worked compared to other parties, particularly the NDP.

Glenn stated he was essentially asking, "I know it's available with the NDP. Is it possible here?" For example, the NDP were known to pay poll captains (the people who canvass door to door), a very rare practice in the Liberal party. It matched how I saw the conversations, if not even more general in nature. Glenn advised the court that my response was that these types of things were doable but nothing was locked down and particularly in exchange for his candidacy.

I had been nauseated and emotional throughout Glenn's time on the stand. It was worse than when the premier testified because Glenn's testimony was more specific to the charges, and the Crown was doing their best to weave the story in a way that somehow got them to evidence. As well, by this point the decision had been made to request a directed verdict (which meant the judge would dismiss the charges before any defence was offered) so every point of confusion might stand in the way of achieving that goal.

The request for a directed verdict came the next day, and a timetable was set. The defence would make its written submission by Friday, September 29. The Crown would take a week and reply one week later, by Friday, October 6. Oral arguments would take place on October 10 and 11 and then the judge would make his decision. We adjourned until Tuesday, October 10, the day after Thanksgiving.

I had argued with my lawyers about the decision to seek a directed verdict. I was concerned we'd be wasting time. Why not just proceed to present our defence and close it down? If we did not win the directed verdict, we'd have to present the defence anyway and wait another few weeks for a final decision. To me, it was all about the fastest route back to the campaign.

Brian set me straight. He was emphatic that if there was ever a case where a directed verdict was warranted, this was it. In his forty-four years as a defence lawyer, he'd only seen a handful of times where a directed verdict was even an option and could count on two hands the number of times he'd been successful. This was the perfect case.

He went a step further. It was unlikely he would recommend presenting a defence. I would prepare to testify in case we needed it and ultimately, the decision was mine to make. Confident we'd reached the threshold of "reasonable doubt," he was unlikely to recommend I testify. Gerry had already said he had no interest in taking the stand. I asked how else I was going to tell my story. He and Erin reminded me that it would never be just my story. The Crown would work hard to disrupt any narrative I believed in. The other point was that if we did not win the directed verdict, the judge would highlight his areas of concern in his written decision. It would provide us the path we'd need to take to get to final verdict of not guilty on both counts.

Lesson: The strength of your convictions will always carry you through.

As the two weeks prior to the directed verdict oral arguments passed, the media stories about the trial had taken a definite turn in our favour. On September 19, Chris Selley of the *National Post* issued my favourite article of the trial to that point, and not just because he used the word "shambolic." Sitting in the courtroom every day, he had a good sense of how the trial was unfolding:

> the Crown's case is so plodding, shambolic and soaked in irrelevancies that I think they've actually managed to move me over to the other side. (Visca puts questions to witnesses the way politicians answer questions from journalists. It's quite remarkable.) When Thibeault says he was just doing exhaustive due diligence before making a huge life decision, it actually rings true.

> … the prosecution's case is a turkey. I've had to scrub the reasonable doubt off me every day when I get back to the hotel. Every witness I've seen on the stand has come off pretty well. There isn't a single embarrassing line in any of the emails in evidence, let alone a smoking gun.

I reviewed the draft directed verdict submission and offered minimal comments. I thought it was amazing and covered what it needed to cover. Anyone wanting a full understanding of the evidence presented, from the defence point of view, should take the time to read it. It was publicly available as soon as it was filed.

The directed verdict oral arguments took place on October 10, 2017. It was a fascinating day, steeped in legalize, but the personalities of the lawyers were on full display. I had been warned that the judge may choose not to engage in a full discussion with lawyers in front of the media but that was not the case. It was a "no holds barred" interchange. Somewhere in the middle of the arguments, I recall the judge saying he had taken over four hundred pages of notes. Even though he had demonstrated the ability to reference back to specific comments made earlier in the trial, I was a bit surprised and very impressed.

It was during these discussions that I began to truly have hope. The judge asked why what occurred would be captured under Section 96 of the *Elections Act*, which covers corruption and bribery. In his words, he summarized that Thibeault wanted two trusted staff to join him and be paid something. Pat responded, "It's doable." The judge stated, "It's not like he said 'I want jobs for my family members or... my friends... These are my two trusted staff.'"

The judge stated it was speculative to suggest that the reason for the conversations with Andrew was that without his support, Glenn might not be willing to be our candidate. The judge made the point that no one had actually put that question to Glenn during his testimony. Visca argued his point rather passionately and somewhat coherently, pointing to the Giroux text as the sole source of his belief that Thibeault was still of the view he needed Andrew to withdraw. The judge called it a weak inference given Glenn's testimony that he knew he'd be the candidate, either by acclamation or appointment.

The judge stated the conversations with Andrew took place for a variety of reasons. We wanted Andrew to withdraw and we wanted the appearance of harmony. Perhaps we wanted Andrew's support. Perhaps to some extent, we wanted to soften the blow, but it appears what we needed most was the appearance of a united front.

Visca argued that on my call with Andrew, I was motivated to keep Glenn in the race. The judge responded, "The more I think about it, the more fanciful it does seem that sort of scenario seems, in anyone's mind, it seems so obvious that by December 11, Thibeault is the candidate, period." The judge asked the Crown how the hiring of the two staff trusted by Glenn could be seen as dishonest and corrupt, or could constitute bribery. The Crown had added the element of "knowingly" to my charge, which could lead to a jail sentence of two years less a day. The judge went out of his way to note that the provision was meant to capture nefarious corrupt practices, not bringing staff onto a campaign.

Crown prosecutor David McKercher chimed in with his view, stating, "What I'm going to suggest is that the… distinction between small bribes and large bribes would be taken into account upon sentencing. A bribe is still a bribe. It's what it boils down to. If… the bribe you want is a new refrigerator, it's still a bribe." His interjection seemed to shock the court, particularly given the tone he took with the judge. A few seconds of stunned silence followed, and I wrote *WTF* in my book.

The judge's reaction: "Yeah. Anything else?"

At the end of the day, the lawyers were relatively confident we had what we needed to achieve a directed verdict on count one. They were less confident about count two given the debate over Glenn's assessment of the commitments made to him and the text from Domenic. It was also about how brave the judge was prepared to be. He could simply go with the "reasonable doubt" scenario and issue a low-risk ruling. But he was fair and open and brave, and he called it as he saw it. We had hope.

We returned to the courtroom on October 24 for what turned out to be the last time. I sat there the day of the directed verdict, having no idea what would happen next. I'd been warned over and over that it was a long shot. The judge entered the room and immediately began reading his verdict.

In his written decision, the judge described a directed verdict as follows: "A directed verdict, or non-suit, will only be granted if the Crown fails to call some evidence on each element of the offence. I look at all of the evidence called, and any reasonable inferences flowing from the evidence and take the Crown's case at its highest." That meant the Crown got the benefit of the doubt, creating a very high bar for a directed verdict. The judge stated that, "Ultimately the question to be answered is whether, based on the evidence and reasonable inferences that flow from the evidence, a reasonable jury, properly instructed, could convict either or any of these charges."

The judge stated his disagreement with the Crown's submission that Andrew was a "candidate" for several reasons. As he listed those reasons, we began to feel count one was breaking our way. On my left, I could sense Erin's excitement. Several pages in, she began to pat my knee (as any outreach had to be out of the court's eye). She then drew a smiley face on her book. I turned slightly and said quietly, "The point or the case?" essentially asking if she was happy with the specific comment the judge was making or the overall outcome. She turned to me and said, "We have it," referring to count one.

Out of the corner of my eye, I saw Michael and Gerry shake hands. It was over for Gerry, but I waited to hear the judge's decision on count two. The emotion was building, and I was holding back tears—tears I still feel to this day. Just a few lines in, I again caught motion to my left and it was Brian closing his notebook. Erin started to pat my knee again and this time I knew she meant it was going very well. I could not really focus on the judge's words any longer as the emotion overwhelmed me, and I put my hands on my knees to stop from shaking. I did catch his final words, "There is no case for her to answer and I direct a verdict of acquittal on all counts for both Ms. Sorbara and Mr. Lougheed."

I remember the judge glancing my way as he said those words. I hoped he could see my gratitude toward him in that moment. I knew I would never be able to publicly thank him given he was only doing his job. And it wasn't that he somehow had let me off the hook. I was grateful for his ability to do his job in a clear-minded way and ignore the politics of it all. He did what no one else had done—not the police, the opposition politicians, the media, not the Crown and certainly not Elections Ontario. He had weighed the details, heard both sides of the story and made a decision based on what had really happened.

I turned to Erin and said, "It's over?"

She replied, "It's over." Unable to hold back the emotion a second longer, I burst into tears, overcome with the tension of the entire trial, and immense relief and joy that it was finally finished. I stood and hugged Erin, Brian, my friend Kathy Robinson, Gerry and Michael. I knew the media and members of the public could see me crying but I didn't care. After hours and hours of keeping it together in that courtroom, I doubted anyone would deny me that moment. I could not bring myself to make eye contact with the Crown who were covering their humiliation by making a show of packing up.

I stood there uncertain about what was to happen next. I then heard Brian and Michael telling the media we'd have a press conference in twenty minutes, in the main foyer. We packed up and headed up to a holding room on the fourth floor to talk strategy.

We discussed what to say and the tone to be used. Michael and Gerry would go first. Gerry pulled a note out of his pocket and indicated he was issuing a statement, as they wanted their position to be clear. We agreed I would keep my comments brief. I would express my gratitude for the verdict and that it was over. I wouldn't get into the details or try to be vengeful.

After Gerry read his statement to the media, Michael added, "I'd be wondering why the money was wasted on the investigation and wasted on the prosecution. It's a day that never should have been. They never should have been subjected to the allegations to begin with."

As we faced the large group of media, Brian was in his element. He defined the verdict as a "clear finding that there simply was no dishonesty, no wrongdoing, no corruption and a clear finding that what was done was done simply in the ordinary course of the work that both Ms. Sorbara and Mr. Lougheed were doing."

I was still shaking from the verdict so it caught me off guard when Rob Ferguson asked how I was feeling and adding, "We could see a few tears up there." I thanked him for pointing that out and moved to the microphones. As we had practised, I said, "I'm grateful this day has come and I kind of always felt it would come... that the law would make the right decision." I later heard from my friend Terrie O'Leary that my performance at the press conference was professional, calm and authentic. I felt good about it, given how little experience I have with answering questions from the media.

I was flying high after the judge issued his directed verdict, feeling totally vindicated. Immediately following my first (and only) press scrum of my political career, I learned the Ontario Liberal Party had issued a press release. I was not consulted on its contents and it expressed the party's long-held confidence that once the facts were known, a court would conclude there was no wrongdoing. Moreover, it stated, "We welcome Pat Sorbara back to the Ontario Liberal campaign and we remain focused on the important work that lies ahead of us." That evening at our celebratory dinner, Brian announced that even though the day represented a massive victory for the legal team, it was that line in the OLP press release that had made him happiest that day.

I later heard that the caucus was together in the Tuesday caucus meeting when they learned of the verdict. The government House leader, Yasir Naqvi, had kept the group together as the decision was being read by the judge. Apparently Yasir had warned the caucus to be muted in their response given the media waiting outside of the caucus room to capture reactions. But they were not to be contained.

We gathered for an evening celebration at the classic Italian Verdicchio Ristorante in Sudbury. Just as we arrived at the restaurant, I was thrilled to take the call I'd been waiting for—my dear friend David Herle. His opening comment was, "You kicked ass." It was a great moment as David and I spoke of how long we'd waited for this chance to look forward to the campaign, knowing we'd again work side by side. I was anxious to pick up life where I'd left off on November 1, 2016. Little did I know how wrong things were about to go.

CHAPTER 11

At the End of the Day, Do Things on Your Own Terms

"If you set out to be liked, you would be prepared to compromise
on anything at any time, and you would achieve nothing."
– MARGARET THATCHER

I saw my one-time boss, former premier David Peterson, in early
May 2018 just a few days before the start of the general campaign.
David and I talked by phone a few times during the Sudbury saga
when he and his wife Shelley called to voice their outrage and offer
support.

He held my hand and said, "Patty, all political careers end in
heartache." (David is one of the only people allowed to call me Patty.
As I could never break him of it, ultimately I came to ignore it.)
Truer words were never spoken. I'd always believed I would be in
control of the circumstances under which I left politics. I'd avoided
the limelight and had rarely been in the media, so it seemed possible. Instead, I faced a reality usually reserved for politicians who
lost elections, or got into trouble somewhere along the way, not the
folks who worked the backrooms. Mine would have ended differently, and much less tragically, except for the friendly fire within my
own party.

*Lesson: Beware of the politics in politics. As you climb the ladder, it's
more and more likely you could be blindsided.*

The day after my return from Sudbury, I sat down with David Herle to talk about how the campaign would run going forward. I didn't want to lose a minute more in getting back to the job. David told me about a meeting that took place about three days before Judge Borenstein was to deliver his decision on our directed verdict application. It was apparently at that meeting that my return to my role was openly discussed for the first time, at least with the premier and the co-chairs in the room. Andrew Bevan raised with the group the concern he had first put on the table in June 2016: senior staff had been unhappy reporting to me and suggested there would be issues if they had to report to me again. Thus began the discussions designed to push me to the edges, if not out.

At one point during the meeting the premier turned to Minister Michael Chan and asked his opinion. Michael is quiet, thoughtful and always measured in his interjections. He responded with a statement and a question. "There's a war out there, right?" The premier responded yes. "And we are losing that war?" Yes. Minister Chan agreed and said, "Then we need our best general on the field and we need her out there now." He was signalling to the premier his view that the priority was running the best possible campaign, not who was winning the personality contest. That story meant a lot to me.

But by the time the co-chairs realized Andrew was following through on a plan to ensure I could not return to the campaign director role, it was much too late. I came to learn over the following weeks he had made a commitment to his cabal of senior staff that they would never have to report to me again. It appeared the strategy was to have me kicked upstairs, leaving Chad Walsh in the role of campaign director. What Andrew did not count on was my refusal to accept a role where the intention was to keep me away from the day-to-day of the campaign.

David, Chad and I met on November 1, 2017. The conversation could not have shocked me more. Most astounding was Chad's declaration that if I was put back in charge, he would leave. I'd sensed something had been wrong since early 2017. As interim campaign director, Chad had rarely reached out with an update or to get advice, which I found unusual and disconcerting given how closely we had worked together before he took over. We were close friends (or so I thought). His distance and silence had been a source of pain and worry. Ultimately, I came to accept that I had little control over what was happening.

It was also during my absence in 2017 that David Clarke was recruited to take over as executive director of the OLP, taking a leave of absence as staff with the Honourable Charles Sousa. He and I sat down to chat not long after he accepted his new role. During that discussion, it became clear to me that no one had told David I would be returning to my role as CEO. I had assumed he'd either return to government or stay on in the executive director role, reporting to me as CEO. David believed he'd been given the role of running the party until after the campaign. After the meeting with David Clarke, I called David Herle from the car, fearful I may have caused a problem. David assured me that regardless of what David Clarke had been told or what he thought, I was coming back—that was not up for debate. It turns out the reason it wasn't up for debate was because no one was talking about it.

Chad was a young man I had worked with side by side for ten years. We met in 2008 during the Rob Oliphant federal campaign, when Chad was a volunteer. When I went to work for Peter Donolo as chief operating officer in the office of the federal Liberal leader of the opposition in 2009, one of my conditions was that Chad be hired. I then hired him at Queen's Park in late 2011, after I went to work as chief of staff to the Minister of Education.

I helped him through every step of his career, happy for him when he became a chief to a minister. As director of organization of the 2014 provincial campaign, he was instrumental to its success. In 2016, I convinced him to leave his role as chief of staff to the Minister of Agriculture to come work in the Premier's Office. Far more important than our work history, Chad was my friend. I trusted him and confided in him. He was a smart, accomplished natural leader. I opened doors and ensured he was given every opportunity to move forward with his political career because I knew he would be a leader in the next generation of the party.

There's no question his accomplishments were his own. My path was different because I was a social introvert who had to work hard to get noticed at a time very few women were in senior roles. Chad was a well-liked, charming and popular extrovert, but he also got the job done. I was demoralized by the realization that somewhere, I had turned from a supportive and encouraging person in Chad's life to an obstacle. I've had many disappointments along the way in politics, but Chad's betrayal of our friendship may be the worst I've experienced. I'm sure he has a side to this story, but he's never shared it with me.

David's assessment of the situation was straightforward: "The Liberal organization wants you back and in charge. It's a bunch of kids who do not..." I remember the moment I realized there had been a second trial—one in which I was definitely not given the opportunity to defend myself. Sitting at home those early days, I reached one conclusion: I was not prepared to give up or give in. The next campaign was just too important. I was not abandoning the people who wanted me at the helm.

On a personal level, I felt strongly that returning to my roles was the most decisive way to put Sudbury behind me, resume my career and undertake a successful political resurrection. I was determined to do just that.

The premier had asked me to attend the senior staff meetings the morning following the meeting with Chad and David. That night, I sent her a text saying it may be mistake given the hostility Chad had emanated earlier that day, along with his reference to other senior staff members feeling the same way. The premier responded that it was important for me to be in the meeting the next morning. I replied that I was disheartened but would be there.

On November 2, two weeks after the directed verdict, I went to a meeting filled with people I'd worked closely with since the 2014 campaign, many whom I called friends. It was there that I realized there was a much deeper movement afoot than Chad Walsh trying to hang onto the title of campaign director. Rebecca Mackenzie, whom I had not seen in more than a year, arrived a few minutes late. I had missed her and felt a surge of joy to see her. As I pushed back my chair, eager to give her a hug, she glanced my way, grimaced and sat down. My heart froze and I choked back tears. I gripped the arm chairs as tight as I could and steadied my breathing. She never looked my way again.

The premier spoke through most of the meeting. She was clear she needed each one of us to be on the team if we were going to win the campaign. No one argued with her, but something was seriously amiss. As senior staff gathered for the next meeting, the premier asked David, me and Chad to come into her office. The premier told Chad she had heard about the meeting the day before and was aware we had a problem. Chad chose to double down. In front of the premier, he suggested it was common knowledge I preferred to operate in an environment of harassment and fear. With every word Chad spoke, I descended deeper into shock and dismay. But the worst was yet to come.

By the time we returned to the premier's boardroom, senior staff had completed their meeting and were waiting for us. Chad had gone in ahead, leaving the premier, David and me to walk in together. I looked around at my fifteen or so colleagues and friends, many of whom I had worked with for years and several I had mentored, suddenly very unsure of myself. A terrible realization dawned as I was greeted with complete silence. Not a single person acknowledged my presence, not a word was spoken, and most looked down at their phones.

The fantasy in my head of being warmly embraced by friends, with applause and cheers of "Welcome back!" faded into fog. Although I thought about running away, it's my nature to stand and fight. The premier, confused, threw her hands in the air and said, "Well, we're here," but her tone asked the question, "What's going on?" I could feel David slightly shaking beside me. No one responded to the premier, and the silence deepened as we sat down, sending a loud message there would be no welcome from this group. There was intent to wound and it worked.

Given the foreboding I had felt in the earlier meeting, I summoned enough courage to just start talking. I told them it warmed my heart to see their faces after so long. As I looked around the room, there was a slight thaw in the ice-cold temperature. When that painful gathering finally ended, a handful of folks congratulated me on the outcome of the trial. I was grateful for a few warm hugs and friendly chatter, making me feel marginally better.

I had never experienced anything so unkind. I felt ostracized and it hurt like hell. I kept thinking these were my friends, people I loved. They had reached out during my absence with offers of support. It was the team I had fought so hard to get back to, the reason winning the case was so vital. My confusion deepened. I went home right after those meetings and tried to think about what to do. I cried more in those next few days than I had during my entire trial.

I attended the OLP provincial council that was happening a few days later in Kitchener. There was about three hundred people there and at one point, I was invited to say a few words. As I looked out over the standing ovation I was given, my heart soared. David's earlier words rang true: the party wanted me back and in charge.

The efforts to turn the premier and co-chairs against me were building. One key example was the premier being told by Chad that Derek Lipman, my long-time colleague and a key organizer for the party, was moving to work with the federal Liberals in Ottawa because he did not want to report to me. I decided to correct the record with the premier, taken aback that she might believe such a thing. I sent a note to the co-chairs and the premier to help them understand there was an effort afoot to undermine me at all costs. It was unusual for me to defend myself in this way, but I was desperate to fight the growing push to get me out.

Although it didn't help much in the long run, I was grateful that Derek clarified his position in writing and made it clear his decision was being used by others as a means to an end. It meant a lot to me that I was not wrong about our working relationship and that we were friends.

Lesson: Don't settle for anything that diminishes who you are or the respect you have earned. At the end of the day, your self-worth is all you have and sometimes the only way to preserve it is to walk away from those who challenge your integrity.

On November 6, there was a second meeting with the premier, David, Chad and me where I was presented with a completely unacceptable job description. It had been written by Andrew, but he was absent from the meeting. I was clear I would not take a role where I did not have the authority to run the campaign. I told the premier I would be okay if she made a different decision, but if she wanted me on the campaign, I had to be in a position to get the job done.

David and I had a few rounds by phone. I kept asking how we got here, and he kept saying he could not do this without me. At one point, angry and frustrated, he asked me just to take the role I was being offered and work it out from there. I was adamant I could not settle for that, a message he took to the premier. Four days later, the premier reached out and we met in person on November 11. For two hours, I walked her through everything I was feeling—and why I should run the campaign.

I told her I was committed to finding a way back to the role, if she still wanted me. She said she did, that she needed my voice at the table. As one of the few senior women around her, she had missed my guidance and input. We agreed to meet again the next day and this time, I insisted Andrew be in the room instead of calling the shots from the outside.

In that meeting, we talked through options around the division of labour between Chad and me. We reached an agreement where I would act in a role similar to the CEO of an organization, with Chad in the role of president. He would direct the day-to-day, but

I would have full oversight and the authority to run the campaign. At the request of the premier, I put the decision and job descriptions into writing and circulated them to the small group. Despite having reached agreement in the meeting with the premier, there continued to be back and forth over several days as we tried to finalize the written document.

The CBC had published an article on November 8 that stated we would "need a significant feat of electoral engineering to pull [an election win] off." I adamantly believed that with my experience, including leading the 2014 campaign, I had the best shot at it. I was driven to work day and night to get it done. I would fight to the political death for Kathleen Wynne, who had stood by me throughout the Sudbury trial. I would be there for the co-chairs who wanted me back. And I would be there particularly for those on the front lines, the committed Liberals and those whose very lives depended on the outcome. I would drive the campaign beyond what anyone believed possible.

Finally on November 21, a document dividing the authority was accepted. It was circulated to the other co-chairs, but not much further. I took the managing co-chair title and Chad would remain campaign director, reporting to me. I agreed to leave much of the day-to-day to Chad, as long as I had oversight authority. I thought it represented a reasonable and workable compromise.

A. Campaign Executive Committee and Campaign Steering Committee

The Co-chairs of the campaign are as follows:

David Herle – Chair of the Executive Committee
Michael Chan
Deb Matthews
Tim Murphy
Patricia Sorbara – Managing Co-chair

The Co-chairs, together with the Campaign Director, form the Campaign Executive Committee. The Campaign Executive Committee is responsible for the overall direction of the campaign and its organization and acts as the Board of Directors for the campaign.

The Campaign Steering Committee, composed of both inside directors who have staff positions within the organization and external directors who are volunteers from outside of the organization, provides input to the Executive Committee and makes decisions specific to the larger issues associated with the campaign.

The Campaign Executive Committee will determine the overall direction and big-picture needs of the organization.

David Herle will continue to act as the individual with overall responsibility for the strategic direction of the campaign.

The Executive Committee delegates responsibility for ensuring the effective execution of the campaign and best possible outcomes to the Managing Co-chair.

B. The Managing Co-chair – Patricia Sorbara

The Managing Co-chair is a member of the Campaign Executive Committee and chairs the Campaign Steering Committee.

She is responsible for integrating the overall strategy, policy and operational direction as determined by the Campaign Executive Committee into the overall operations of the campaign. She will be involved and interact with the campaign staff and machinery regularly and as necessary. Direction from the Managing Co-chair will be provided to the Campaign Director and from there to the members of the campaign operations team.

As the top decision-maker focused on the vision and strategy of the organization, the Managing Co-chair provides regular reports to the Campaign Executive Committee and Campaign Steering Committee, updating them on the overall progress of set goals and campaign readiness.

Working directly with and through the Campaign Director, she is responsible to ensure effective outcomes of the strategies and plans being implemented including:

- Approval of and direction to Campaign Director on working structure, the establishment of process and protocols, lines of authority and reporting relationships;
- All elements of the campaign are designed to fulfil the operational and strategic direction of the campaign and meet priorities;
- Monitor the competition, ensuring both an offensive and defensive strategy;
- Oversee the pre-writ and in-writ budget, in coordination with the Ontario Liberal Party Executive Director;
- Ensure the organization is meeting needed targets for revenue generation, in coordination with Ontario Liberal Party; and
- Ensure the critical path is current and it is being executed effectively, both in terms of the short and long-term goals;

C. The Campaign Director – Chad Walsh

The Campaign Director reports to the Managing Co-chair and is a member of the Campaign Steering Committee and Campaign Executive Committee.

He directs and manages the individuals responsible to execute each of the line areas of operation within the campaign. His focus is on the execution of the elements of the campaign including specific tasks, duties and responsibilities. He is responsible for the day-to-day operations and excellence in execution.

Working with the directors in each area of the campaign, the campaign director will oversee all outcomes through:

- Creation, updating and execution of the critical path of the campaign including tactical and operational aspects of the strategy and daily functions of the organization;
- In consultation with the Managing Co-chair, plan and initiate the execution of the strategy determined by the Executive Committee;
- Manage and direct the day-to-day affairs of the campaign team and oversee and provide direction to staff.
- Oversee the outreach to local campaigns, ensuring their needs are met and they achieve a mission-critical level of readiness;
- Ensures professionalism, operational excellence, organizational efficiency and productivity;
- Ensures the elements required for success are in place by implementing objectives and establishing a framework for executing the details associated with key initiatives; and,

- Ensures the campaign is working smoothly by managing the many elements that make up the organization, including the requirements of its broad volunteer base.

Following its release, there were several notes of congratulations and expressions of relief. Tim Murphy commented, "Great to have Pat back and great to have our campaign organization lead by two such talented team members as Pat and Chad!"

It turned out to be a pipe dream. I should have realized earlier that the intent to move me out was not going to be stopped by a simple document. The isolation of being away from the Centre for a year had done its job. It made sense that people naturally began to fill the gaps left by my absence.

From time to time, I wonder if I should have accepted the lesser role. I reach the same conclusion each time. It would have resulted in constant conflict, with me fighting to be at the table of the real decisions. It would have meant going back to the world I lived in after Andrew took over control of the Premier's Office. It would have meant non-stop office politics. And I would not have been able to do the work we needed to get done.

Lesson: Political organizations have a culture. They can build you up or tear you down. But never underestimate how far you can get with a positive mindset.

In a true partnership with Chad, the campaign could have worked well. I told the premier I was ready to pass the baton to the next generation but in this campaign, the oversight of a seasoned professional was critical. More importantly, it greatly needed the discipline and accountability I would put in place. It was becoming clear with each passing day that the rearguard action was not going to stop. With Andrew supporting the front line who said they would not work with me, it was inevitable that I would be gone. But I tried. I wanted only to move forward.

I threw myself into the work. I went to every meeting I could get into but that in and of itself proved a hurdle. I could not get anyone to tell me when the meetings were, let alone get myself invited to them. I finally came to realize that, just five short months before the election would be called, there had been little to no organization around the campaign. And where it existed, there was a concentrated effort to keep me at a distance.

Regardless, I started to move a number of issues forward quickly. I spent a lot of time with staff who came to me to talk about their concerns and areas of the campaign that were falling behind.

There was perhaps no better example than the mission-critical work we were doing with Data Sciences. In 2014, their efforts to convert our database system to Liberalist was instrumental to our win. It had been the first step on the transition to modern campaigning, giving us the ability to make data-driven decisions. I had finalized a deal with them to ensure that by 2018, we were positioned emulate the highly successful outreach campaign executed by the federal Liberals in 2015. Immediately upon my return, it was evident the project had fallen well behind the targets and, without a significant push, it wasn't going to be ready. The very large financial investment was at risk. The individuals running the program on behalf of OLP raised the alarm, as did Tom Pitfield, the founder and CEO of Data Sciences. (He was amongst the happiest and most relieved to see me back.) Tom and his most senior people came immediately to the table to urgently put into place a critical path to meet the needed milestones. I was given a foundational briefing and we began weekly meetings and daily calls. Within a few weeks, everyone felt we might just pull it off.

I began to attend the morning calls with the premier as well as the daily senior staff meetings. I worked to signal we'd moved into a world of "business as usual" but it felt very different. My efforts to integrate and address issues continued to be strongly resisted by the core group around Andrew (and thus around the premier) who also had senior roles in the campaign.

One of the shocks I experienced upon my return was the culture shift that had taken place since my departure in November 2016. It was now over a year later and the attitudes being exhibited by the senior people running the government and the party were negative, unkind and focused on who was in charge rather than the task ahead. I learned that Moira McIntyre, who replaced me as deputy chief of staff, referred to staff who had worked with me and wanted to work with me again as "Pat Rats." She made sure they were isolated from the day-to-day operations and withheld information she was fearful they might share with me.

Just before Christmas, the next volley of attacks began. Nominations commissioner Alexis Levine emailed the premier directly and threatened to resign his role. A very close friend of Chad's, Alexis was causing me incredible grief. Although his role required neutrality, he was the least neutral person sitting at the candidate search table. I began to bring the co-chairs into more of the decisions being made by the candidate search committee, ensuring the views of others were considered. It meant Alexis was no longer able to call the shots without being challenged, and he did not like it.

Alexis gave the premier an ultimatum: unless she fired me, he would resign. I called Alexis and asked him to stay, saying we could find a way to work together. Ultimately the premier called Alexis and said while she wanted him to stay, she was not prepared to accept his ultimatum. I was grateful for that show of confidence.

The premier had also asked David if he felt I'd be willing to get some coaching around my management style and working through the challenges that were clearly ahead. When David raised it with me, I immediately said yes. I knew the value of a sounding board, someone to provide objective perspective and a place to take your emotions. That brought the amazing coach Silvia Presenza back into my life. I had met her in the 1990s when she worked for MPP Michael Colle. The fit was great because she understood politics and she knew David.

We met two or three times and I knew it was going to help a lot. I told her I wanted to be a better manager and address the issues at the heart of people's concerns. It made me think again about the disconnect that was happening. My management style has been the same for decades. I am hard-driving, I insist on discipline and accountability. Deadlines are met. If you can't meet the deadline, we work together to figure out how to manage the gap. If you want responsibility and you demonstrate you can handle it, you get it.

I don't know any other way to effectively manage a large, complex, layered organization with a looming, non-negotiable deadline on the horizon. The co-chairs and people who did not work at Queen's Park but had senior roles in the campaign knew that discipline and focus had been missing and looked to me to ensure it happened.

One of the ideas I discussed with the premier and with Silvia was to sit down with the key people leading the teams and clear the air. We'd have a mediated, open discussion. People could tell me how they felt, and I would be given the chance to respond. Where necessary, I would apologize and assure the team we could do this differently. But others felt it was a bad idea: the debate needed to be over and we needed to get to work within the approved structure. I think it was a missed opportunity and likely the only one that may have made a difference to the outcome.

Lesson: Be prepared to draw a line, no matter how painful. And if the time comes that you have to go, never take the party down with you.

Alexis formally resigned on January 15 and took several of the volunteers who formed the candidate vetting committee with him. Many of them I did not know, nor had I worked with them. I could only assume they left in solidarity with Alexis. Andrew responded that we needed to take action to stop the "exodus of good people from the campaign."

David, Chad and I met that morning and in David's view it went well—but I felt false positivity in the room. David assured me he would talk with Chad to confirm there were no issues that needed to be addressed around the new structure. I urged him to do it soon, my senses on high alert.

Chad resigned the next morning. He sent his resignation note to only David and Andrew, again making the point he wasn't prepared to follow the new structure. He stated that his role in the campaign had become managing the people who were unhappy I was in charge. He said he'd spent three hours of his first day back from holiday dealing with complaints about the way I'd handled meetings the previous week. There were no details and nothing to which I could respond. He reiterated that he wanted no part of the environment in which I operated. We suspended the riding-by-riding review that was underway, and David headed to see the premier. Once again, I was left out of the dialogue with her.

There were a number of discussions over the next day and word about the resignations was getting out. Media questions started to surface. We were going to need a strategy and fast. David and I had a long talk about what it meant should Chad follow through on the resignation. I told him that honestly I would be relieved: all the duplicity would come to an end and the debate would be over; I would work to fill in the blanks and we'd build a team focused only on a successful campaign. I would have been happy to work with Chad but that clearly wasn't going to happen.

The five co-chairs met for dinner on January 17. There was concern around what would happen next but there was unanimous agreement on one thing: I was to stay in the role, with the authority to run the campaign. Deb Matthews called the premier after the meeting to tell her of the co-chairs' decision. The premier said she'd need to sleep on it.

What we did not know at the time was that there were more resignations put to the premier. I don't know the full details but with what I've been able to piece together, at least one other senior staff person, Mel Wright, indicated her intent to resign. As well, Chad signalled his resignation was not only from his role with the campaign but also his position in the Premier's Office. Andrew may have also told the premier he would have to leave, given that he had made the original commitment to senior staff that I'd not be back in my role. Whatever the specifics, it proved too much pressure. The premier made the decision to overrule her co-chairs.

The next morning, I had a very bad feeling. I had not heard from anyone and neither Deb nor David were answering their phones. Finally, I got a call back from David. I asked him what was happening, and he said, "It's bad." I asked how bad and he replied, "The worst." I was out. The premier decided I had to leave the campaign.

Shortly thereafter a call came from Carly Foerster, the executive assistant to the premier. She asked that I come to Queen's Park at eleven a.m. to meet with the premier. Aware cabinet was meeting, my assistant Mike Johnson spoke with her and said I was not coming over. He was clear I was not walking through senior civil servants, political staff and the media who would be gathered outside the cabinet room, to meet with the premier in her office so she could fire me.

Carly was unaware of the situation, but once Mike explained the circumstances, she kindly went to the premier and made alternate arrangements. The premier left the cabinet meeting and headed to OLP. As the premier walked past OLP staff, their shock registered at this highly unusual scenario. She entered my office, sat down and said, "I'm going to need that resignation." I told her I wasn't going to resign because I was not prepared to walk away from the party, nor was I prepared to signal that the trial had defeated me.

In reminding me that I had indicated in the past that I would resign if she asked me to, I responded that the circumstances were quite different and always in the context of Sudbury. She said firmly, "Well, I'm not going to fire you." And while that was exactly what was happening, I agreed it should not be the public message. We eventually came to ground on what was essentially the truth—the problems trying to re-integrate into the team were just too major to overcome. That settled, the premier said to me, "This is the worst political day of my life."

I replied with sadness and some anger, "Well, it's likely to be the last political day of mine." What I thought about but did not say was that my only goal was to ensure that June 7 was not the worst political day of her life—how prophetic that turned out to be. It also occurred to me, as I said to many others afterward, that the cabal of senior staff around her had achieved what the PCS, NDP, OPP, Elections Ontario and the Crown prosecutors could not—I was out.

I knew the premier was heartsick. I was too. I wasn't going to make it any tougher on either of us than it needed to be. We shared an embrace and she returned to the cabinet meeting. I heard later that she told the ministers she had let someone go from the campaign; many said she was tearful as she left the cabinet room.

I asked David Clarke to gather the OLP staff in the boardroom. I was really in no shape to talk but this moment was important to me. When I was charged on November 1, 2016, I was not given the chance to say goodbye and I wasn't going to let that happen again. Through many tears, I thanked them for letting me be part of their team and told them I had been asked to leave the campaign. I said I had wanted to face this challenge with them, that they were the best and to never give up. I packed up what I could carry and Mike drove me home. I called Peter Donolo who kindly stepped in on my behalf to negotiate the wording in the public statement. Eventually the statement was issued as follows:

STATEMENT FROM THE PREMIER

As you know, while Pat Sorbara was gone from the Ontario Liberal Party to deal with the Elections Ontario charges in Sudbury, we continued our hard work getting ready for the 2018 campaign.

Recently there has a been a great deal of discussion about the structure of the campaign team moving forward. Pat Sorbara will not be joining the campaign team. However, I will continue to count upon her personal friendship.

The team that stepped up while Pat was forced to deal with completely unfounded charges in Sudbury came together and gelled in the last several months. This is the team that will take us into the coming election. The full organizational structure for the campaign will be announced in the near future.

We have a lot of hard work to do as we move forward on our plan to create more fairness and opportunity for everyone in Ontario, and I have full confidence in the talent and experience of our campaign team.

The media reached out to me for a statement. Many of them I knew from Queen's Park and some from the trial. I decided I would not comment, as my goal was never to hurt the premier or the campaign. Instead, after hearing a lot of different versions around what had happened on January 20, I sent out a series of tweets to set the record straight. They read:

> Two things I know for sure about politics: 1) it is not for the faint of heart and 2) if you work as political staff, you serve at the pleasure of the Leader.

> For the past 3 years, fall out from the #Sudbury by-election impacted me deeply, on many levels. What kept me going the entire time was an intense desire to return to help @KathleenWynne and the @OntLiberal team fight to win the 2018 election.

> Buoyed by the unequivocal judgement that there had been no wrongdoing, I did just that. But issues re-integrating into the existing team proved too tough to overcome. The Leader made the decision she felt best and I am no longer part of the campaign.

> I am very saddened by her decision but I defend the Leader's right to make it. Another thing I know about politics is sometimes tough calls are unavoidable.

I wish Premier @KathleenWynne & everyone in the campaign all the best. Truly. I often say there is life after politics. I will find my way forward because one thing I know
for sure, I am not faint of heart.

I also changed my Twitter bio to read, *Nellie McClung: 'Never retreat,
never explain, never apologize. Get the thing done and let them howl"
Longtime political operative. Liberal. Always.*

Shortly following my departure, there was a campaign retreat. I
had been planning it and it went ahead. I talked with Silvia and with
her help prepared the following email which I sent to the senior
campaign team on January 27:

Hello All:

Beyond everything that has happened since I returned to
the campaign team after a year away, I wanted to reach
out to you on a personal level. My mind wanders often to
the long relationship I've had with most of you, as work
colleagues and in many cases, as my friends.

I want to begin by saying I'm sorry. I've had to hear some
difficult feedback about how people often felt when working with me. These experiences were not what I ever intended and I am filled with regret and sadness. Please
know that I only ever wanted to see everyone do their best
but I understand that in the process, I did not always do my
best. Going forward I am committed to learning from this
and doing better.

This leads me to the other reason for this note. I want
to wish you all the best, personally and professionally.
We share the desire to do our very best and to work our
hardest to ensure Kathleen Wynne is re-elected in June,

in support our caucus and candidates, the Ontario Liberal Party and the people of the province. For me that means accepting the decision I cannot be part of this campaign team. For you, it means becoming a team united and ready for the fight ahead.

Please know I will be rooting for you from the sidelines. And if I can ever be of help to you, please don't hesitate to reach out.

Warmest regards and all the best. Pat

The note was important, and I meant every word of it. At the same time, Silvia and I agreed that I did not have to apologize for expecting people to be competent, accountable and responsible. She reminded me the note was a powerful way to demonstrate my unrelenting commitment to the party and the team, as well as my professionalism.

I sat at home and worked to accept the reality of it all. Months later, I came to accept a few basic tenets around what happened. I was the victim of friendly fire, an internal mob hit. Cold and calculated, planned out and executed by a few who placed their own needs over that of the campaign and the party. In the book *Shattered*, about all that went wrong with the Hillary Clinton campaign, there is a reference to campaign manager Robert Mook that noted that he had "a desire to maintain the kingdom rather than win the war." I felt it highly applicable to Andrew and his cabal.

Over the years when I could tell people found my hard-driving style to be a challenge, I would smile and say to them, "You'll miss me when I am gone." They may have wanted the job done but did not want to put in the hard work or meet the deadlines. I think those words were proven true during the lead-up to the 2018 campaign.

When all of this began, I pulled a book from my bookshelf. It was Timothy Findley's *Not Wanted on the Voyage*. It is basically the story of Noah's Ark and the prologue gave a sense of how I was feeling: "To begin with, they made it sound as if there wasn't any argument; as if there wasn't any panic—no one was being pushed aside... They also made it sound like there wasn't any dread... Flags and banners and a booming cannon... like an excursion. Well. It wasn't an excursion. It was the end of the world."

It's how I felt about the coming campaign. It wasn't some excursion and we weren't fighting over who was going to captain the ship. We were looking at the end of our world. And end it did. The senior staff around the premier put their own interests ahead of hers and ahead of party. The premier made a decision that directly impacted the party and the candidates who had stepped forward to run for us. In the end, the party paid a very big price.

My political career ended. I sat at home and watched the campaign unfold, thinking about Kathleen Wynne and what had happened to her and her government. And watched the Ontario Liberal Party fall further than I ever thought possible.

CHAPTER 12

Politics is a Roller Coaster, So Be Prepared for the Highs and the Lows

"You can't wring your hands and roll up your sleeves at the same time."

– MICHELE BROWN

I've been asked over and over again: what happened in the 2018 campaign that would cause the Liberals to fail so badly? How had Kathleen Wynne become one of the most unpopular Canadian politicians of all time? For a long time, and certainly since I was benched, I've thought about those questions. Some days I thought about little else.

There were other losses, too, that were changing the political landscape. For 277 days in 2013 (February 11 to November 13), Canada had the greatest number of female first ministers in its history. Six of the country's thirteen premiers were women. Approximately 88 percent of Canadians had a female provincial leader. It was a notable moment in the breaking of the glass ceiling, and a time of incredible hope within the women's movement. But in the end it was unsustainable. Just as I finished writing this book, on April 16, 2019, Canada's last female premier standing, Rachel Notley of Alberta (who'd been elected in 2015), fell to defeat. On top of that, the country appears to be tacking right as provincial Liberal governments are being overturned at regular intervals, with most losing to the Conservatives.

And in the backrooms, the approach to campaigning is changing drastically, particularly in the context of voter outreach. Modern campaigning means targeting specific messages to specific voters by candidates, parties and third-party organizations. It requires a strategy and money. Apparently some believe it requires a willingness to mislead, stoke fear and play the politics of division.

All of this context is important because in some ways, Kathleen Wynne was just one of many leaders of a long-time government defeated by the change narrative. When you've been in politics long enough, you come to understand it as a cycle. As communications strategist Jaime Watt reminded me, when the Liberal party was tanking in the polls in 2018, the OLP had simply come to the end of its cycle. It will rise again, recover and live to fight another day. I know he's right because I was there in 2011 when the federal Liberal party suffered a crushing defeat, causing many to predict we'd wander in the wilderness for years to come. But just four years later, the Liberals formed government on a change mandate when the country had finally had enough of Stephen Harper.

I can only speak to what I witnessed when I worked directly with the government and the party, as well as what I learned from the many people I talked with who were both on the ground and in the central campaign. It was a campaign in which the OLP was not only defeated but yielded its worst outcome since Confederation, including the loss of party status in the legislative assembly.

So what happened? The issues are layered and complex, and it went beyond what women in politics face every day. I believe it was both about the expectations the voters had of Kathleen Wynne because she was a woman, but more significantly about who she was as a premier. In the end, we failed to deliver on the expectation that the first woman premier would be the change. There would be no second chance. There's no single answer but there are important lessons. In trying to understand what happened, the larger context of the state of the OLP must be factored in as well as the political environment of the day.

Lesson: In politics it's always best to deliver on what you've sold. A disappointed electorate who feels duped won't hesitate to mete out punishment.

The person who made the decision to sell off a government asset and seemingly ignore the plight of those suffering from the impact of high hydro bills was in no way the person the voters believed they had elected. Their confusion and unhappiness gave way to a sense of betrayal and ultimately a visceral dislike of Kathleen Wynne. This was not the Kathleen Wynne who told them she'd be the change.

Voters were unable to reconcile their expectations of this premier with this decision. She had not acted in a consultative way despite her commitment to do so. She ignored their very vocal concerns, appearing to no longer care what they thought. It pointed to what made them disdainful of politicians. But it was worse because they had believed this woman would act differently from what they considered the norm.

There was a serious dichotomy between how the public eventually saw Kathleen Wynne and how she was seen over her many years as an elected official by the members of the Ontario Liberal Party, her caucus, her senior staff and the large number of political staffers who worked in government and for the party. It was not just about electoral success. She was and still is truly beloved within our party because she cares about people, as individuals. She was present at weddings and met many new babies. When she heard of personal issues, she tried to help find a solution. Despite being in the midst of the Sudbury saga, she attended my mom's funeral and once stopped a meeting to announce the arrival of my youngest great-niece.

Four days before election day on June 7, 2018, I watched the news as Kathleen Wynne, leader of the Ontario Liberal Party, purposefully walked to a podium and rewrote the campaign playbook. She took what some called the unprecedented step of telling the world that she knew she could not win the election, without apology or explanation. It was what it was, and in her practical way, she called the next play by admitting her team was not going to win the war, but we'd continue to fight local battles.

For me it was vintage Kathleen Wynne. It was the Kathleen I wished we had seen more of throughout her years as premier. The campaign leadership had told her about a week earlier that internal polling confirmed what the external polls were indicating. The Liberals were not only in a fight for party status, but in fact faced complete annihilation. I know she would have internalized that information and come to her own decision on how best to proceed. Pretending was generally not in her nature. So, she called it. That was the person the voters elected in 2014 and had lost sight of along the way.

Lesson: It's been said that, "You can only dodge for so long—eventually you have to throw a punch." Government tends to sit back and take a pounding because it's expected to stay above the fray. Sometimes though, you have to stand up to the schoolyard bullies.

The Kathleen Wynne I know has sharp elbows, but tended to use them only when she felt she was left with little choice; I saw it more than once. But as premier, Kathleen was rarely allowed to go after her opponents or land a punch, even though she was quite capable of it. Rather than be herself, she had to act "like a premier." I worried that it confused people when she defended the government and the issues, using facts and figures, but she rarely defended herself. Eventually the debate around letting her fight back became irrelevant; government was so disliked that we lacked the moral authority to call out the opposition.

All of this was perhaps surmountable and it's unsure how it contributed to the single largest issue that brought down the Liberal government: deep and unrelenting dislike (some would argue "hatred") of Kathleen Wynne—to the point that they would vote for anyone over Premier Wynne—even Doug Ford (who some would say acts less "like a premier" than anyone who has ever held the position).

Over the past few years, many have waited for the clouds to part and the sun to shine on a simple answer that would show what we'd all somehow missed. It proved impossible to figure it out, at least using the traditional methods, including polling and focus groups. We talked with people who knew Kathleen well and asked what changes they might have noticed to bring about such dislike from the public. We were at a loss.

The general public appears to have reached a conclusion that at the end of the day, Kathleen Wynne did not care about them. She was part of the traditional political elite and not a true representative of change. They trusted her to be different, but she wasn't. We had built their expectations to the point that a fall from that height simply could not be survived. I believe it could have been different, right from the start. Or even from the middle.

Lesson: When things aren't working, it's time to step back, assess and make the needed changes. There will be sacrifices but sometimes drastic change is the only option.

I always liked and appreciated the saying, "You can't see the forest for the trees." But where, in fact, can you ever see the forest? It certainly is not when you are standing in its midst, no matter how magnificent. Or walking through it, you spend much of your time looking down to avoid tripping over tree stumps or looking around to admire the creatures of the forest. To truly see a forest in its entirety, you have to get above it.

We seemed never to get above it. One thing for sure is we would have had to slow down. I realize that's not the nature of government but any hope of winning the long game would have required doing less but doing it exceptionally well. Each decision would have gone forward only after exhaustive consultation, input from cabinet and caucus and a roll-out plan designed to ensure the desired impact could be achieved. And critically, a communications strategy that positioned us to sustain the key messaging around every decision.

I am a big planner, which many people find annoying because it means a lot of meetings and a constant review of the plans until issues are resolved and are ready for implementation. I believe it could have made all the difference. We needed to step back from the day-to-day chaos and design a plan, a plan based on understanding how our efforts as a government would be measured against the electorate's primary expectation of us—*be the change*. And then we needed to work as a team to create a road map to get us through the four years ahead of us.

How amazing would it have been to conduct interviews immediately post-election in 2014 to ask people why they voted for Kathleen Wynne and the Liberals? What kind of change did people believe they were going to get? It would have meant being different in all the ways government interacted with the public. Heading the list would have been consulting and communicating in a way very outside of the box, including preconditioning the public and responding to issues and concerns prior to taking any action considered final. It would have taken time, but it would have been far more likely to create a positive outcome.

It would have meant giving Kathleen Wynne time to think, to check her gut, to decide what she wanted to say and do; to give her input into every speech so it reflected how she really felt about something, not what others thought people needed to hear from her. To do that, we'd have had to reduce the number of major events and build more private time into the schedule. That would have been tough on a lot of levels, including Kathleen's tendency to always be available, but it would have paid dividends in terms of ensuring that positive outcomes could be sustained. I believe Kathleen also would have benefited from a small group of key advisors who formed her "kitchen cabinet," much like she had in the 2014 election, with the mandate that everyone would be able to speak freely. I'm not entirely sure what happened while I was away from the team, but my sense was that the premier never again had a cohesive core group around her. Toward the end of the mandate, the premier began to seek advice from different people at a time she should have been anchored by a small group of key advisors who had only one agenda—to protect her.

By the end of my time in the Premier's Office, I believed Andrew Bevan's goal was to be the only voice in the premier's head. From my perspective he was successful. If he wasn't the one talking to her, it was one of the senior staff members who followed his direction. The more unstable we became as a government, the more the Centre took control. A few others had limited input. Sometimes a senior cabinet minister, senior staff member or occasionally an outside advisor like Ed Clark was allowed in, but rarely.

And then there was the team. I was distressed (at times even distraught) by the change in the culture I saw happening within the Liberal organization at Queen's Park. Over the five years we'd been in power, there was a concentrated effort to make the political role of staff more about the job of a government public servant and less about being political. Shelley Potter talked about "making it a more professional environment," which in my mind was code for making it more bureaucratic. As a result, the political work became less critical in the minds of many.

The impact on staff was evident. They were less motivated to be part of the political movement they were hired to support: to help in by-elections, to be contributors and to attend party events. At a time when all parts of the organization should have worked in tandem, the party became estranged from the government and vice versa. It felt to me that we were losing focus on the political side of our job.

It was partly due to that bureaucratic approach that so many of our best went to Ottawa to work with the federal Liberals. And when they did, instead of thanking them for being the outstanding staffers they had been, they were treated poorly. They deserved better. And given it was those people to whom we'd turn to for help when our election came around again, that poor treatment was unnecessary and short-sighted.

There are those who say that the work in government must be separated from the work in politics. I don't believe that. As long as the people who run the government are politicians who seek re-election every four years, it will never work that way. The reality is that political staff are there to do the work of politics and should be transparent about it. They will execute their government roles very well, but always with an eye to the political reality of the day.

The one comment that always elicited an immediate and sharp response from me was, "You are paid political staff, so you have no choice but to be here." Whether it was said by a party volunteer or a member of the public, it would draw my ire. Nothing could be further from the truth. Political staff are there because they believe in the cause; they do their jobs and then some, and when it's necessary, they do even more—whatever it takes. They show up when no else is available and do the work no one else wants to do. The suggestion that political staff are motivated by the job or the money or the prestige is unacceptable to me because I know differently; it is the cause and what they can contribute to that cause. As such, when some in the Premier's Office began to treat staff in that same way, I found it upsetting and offensive.

Loyalty in politics is a two-way street. I never made anyone feel badly about leaving politics and I did what I could to ensure they did not lose out financially. When we were crushed in Ottawa, I worked with the human resources department to manage the situation around each staff person, doing the best we could for each individual. Many political staff at Queen's Park no longer felt like the leadership cared about them in the way previous Liberal governments had. There's much that can be done for staff who give up weekends, evenings and holidays to work on the political side of the party. We started to fail at doing those things.

Lesson: Leaders come and go. At the end of the day, there is always the party.

Many times, I raised with the premier the less than desirable state of the party. For years the party office had suffered as the poor cousins to the people who worked in government. The OLP executive director would make an excellent hire only to have that person stolen away a few months later to work for a minister or an MPP. In my mind the less than ideal physical conditions in which they worked reflected their status in the party. And yet when all was said and done, they would be the entity left standing should the election not go well.

I argued that re-election would require approaching the fight as if we were a hungry opposition seeking to gain government. And that meant that the party had to be strong enough to carry the lion's share of the effort. To get to that level of readiness, we needed Kathleen Wynne to be the leader of the party and not just the premier. At the end of the day, the party did not get much attention from her as other priorities always got in the way. There was little inspiration or direction. There were few meetings with the OLP executive branch, and the relationship was uneasy. Outreach to the rank and file was minimal. Liberal events were the last to make it onto the schedule and the first to be cut.

I had hoped there would be an effort to build the party up. Instead, her speeches at the annual general meeting and pre-campaign rallies spoke to how well our government was doing rather than a call to arms. Meanwhile our party was broke and lacked organization, and campaign readiness had lagged. We did talk about how bad things were getting—at meetings of campaign committee, senior staff, caucus—but never in a way that allowed people to exhibit the panic or anxiety they truly felt. We all played along with the belief that because we were a good government we could turn it around during a campaign, but we stood by and watched as the strength of the party diminished.

Lesson: Accept when it's time to save the furniture and act accordingly.

The reality is that when the election got underway on May 7, 2018, Premier Kathleen Wynne headed a Liberal government that had been in place for fourteen years and six months. These days that's an exceptionally long time for a party to stay in power. In both 2011 and 2014, the Liberal Party pulled off unexpected wins. But with the rocky four years we'd had, at the start the 2018 campaign the public saw us as a dead-in-the-water government and the party was virtually on life support.

I attended the OLP provincial council at the end of September 2018, over three months after the election. There was a poignant moment when a campaign worker from a riding stepped to the microphone and asked the campaign co-chairs seated across the stage a single question, "Why didn't you tell us how badly it was going?" From all I had heard and seen, that summed up the 2018 campaign. It was approached as though the Liberals had a chance to win, not to fight for as many seats as we could hold onto, which was the only thing that made sense given the political environment. Although I left in mid-January, I heard regularly from friends, staff and local Liberals asking for my help and advice, or just needing to tell me they were scared and uncertain, and had no idea what to do next. I encouraged them to talk with the central campaign and their regional advisors. There was little else I could do.

Local campaigns were completely blindsided when Kathleen Wynne told the country that the Liberals would not be re-elected. It was so out of the blue that some candidates learned of it as they canvassed that Saturday morning from voters who'd just seen it on television. Up to that point, ridings had not been told what was happening in their area or across the province. As a result, they had not developed a battle plan that would give them the best chance of surviving the tsunami coming at them.

It would have required a wholesale shift away from the leader-based campaign to one entirely focused on local campaigns and candidates. No direction was provided, no messaging, no literature. And as it was just four days before election day, it was simply too late in the game to move the fight to the riding level. Despite that reality, the day before the election I talked to candidates who believed their local popularity would win the day. It was not to be.

Campaign managers told me that when they asked the Centre what was happening in their area, the response they'd get was, "It's not looking good in the southwest," or "It's tough in the North." The central campaign refused to provide the details we had made available to ridings in 2014. That approach seriously underestimated the ability of the front-line campaigns, who already sensed they were losing, to accept reality (no matter how bad it was going to be) and create a local strategy to fight it through to the end.

David Herle responded to the question of why the Centre did not tell ridings how bad things had become by saying they did not want to demoralize the candidates and workers. David always believed there was a path to success and he never stopped searching for it. He called his peers and considered every single option he could find. He blamed himself when he could not find one. The reality is that in 2018 there may not have been a way through. But an earlier acknowledgement of what was really happening likely would have made it possible to save more ridings.

Lesson: When you are no longer winning the war, you move to a battle-by-battle scenario. You go back to the basics and rebuild the base: one person at a time, one vote at the time.

It felt to some that with all going wrong with the air war, the ground war was also abandoned. There was an ongoing debate about running television and radio ads as opposed to putting what remaining budget was available into targeted and riding-specific outreach via social media. It was a good example of something that should have been decided well before the campaign even started. We would have agreed in advance the parameters around which we'd move away from less-flexible, traditional advertising and focus on micro-targeted outreach through Data Sciences, the more effective and efficient way to influence local voters.

When I returned to work at the end of 2017, it was immediately obvious that election readiness was nowhere near what it needed to be five months before the election. Many confirmed that after I was pushed out, there continued to be very little progress. We went into the campaign with a slate of candidates but little else. Things were certainly not at the pitch-perfect level we would have needed to take on the massive fight we faced. It seemed we acted like winning a fifth mandate could be approached the same way as winning a second.

Two years out we should have begun the process to target which ridings were winnable and focus attention there. Local candidates and campaigns should have been measured against their pre-writ readiness efforts and resources assigned accordingly. There was some work being done but it was patchy and undisciplined; local campaigns were not monitored closely enough, with actual data, to know which ridings were ready and which were not.

In his book *Campaign Confessions: Tales from the War Rooms of Politics*, John Laschinger, one of a few career campaign managers in Canada, stated, "Lack of discipline on a campaign team is a prescription for disaster." He also said that it is at a time of low expectations that you should take risks and think outside the box. Both of those statements rang true for me as I heard about the operations around the 2018 campaign. Like the way we ran government, the OLP approached the election in the most traditional way possible.

Political staff were assigned to ridings that were not only unwinnable in the 2018 circumstances, they would have been a remote possibility at any time. At the post-election provincial council, Deb Matthews was surprised by the boos from the audience when she suggested that the central campaign had stayed in touch with ridings. I heard from so many campaigns that they felt there was nowhere to turn for help. Others said the campaign office was barely staffed in the evenings when local campaigns were the busiest.

Above all, we had no business running a ground game based on a belief we could win government again. Maybe we could have gotten there with an outstanding, flawless campaign but for two years the numbers had indicated we were going to lose seats and likely a lot of them. The reality was it was time to save the furniture. I understood what David and others told me after the campaign—we were just trying to win an election. But all indications had been that a fifth mandate was not in the cards and instead we faced decimation.

While the Liberals were trying every option they could think of, constantly manoeuvring in the hopes of finding a message that would resonate, the Conservatives were in stealth mode. There was no platform, few policies but many platitudes, the key one being "We're not Kathleen Wynne." The leader's tour was minimalist, representing an aggressive attempt to hide their leader Doug Ford. Their candidates were no-shows at local all-candidate meetings. The general approach of "Nothing to look at here, folks," was designed to avoid a mistake that would force the electorate to think carefully about their inclination to vote for the person they thought most likely to defeat the Liberal government. And it worked. Claiming to be "for the people," the Tories asked for blind support, and they got it.

The NDP began strong and in the first few weeks of the campaign, looked positioned to pull off a win. Andrea Horwath projected a leader who was fair-minded, thoughtful and inclusive. Liberal ads aimed at driving people away from Doug Ford and back to the Liberals instead drove voters to the NDP, inadvertently contributing to a mid-campaign NDP surge. After her solid performance at the first debate, Horwath began to ride a wave. But then came the bad news in the form of self-inflicted wounds caused by a failure to fully screen candidates, and a war room that appeared unprepared for the inevitable attacks on their leader.

Above all, Horwath's insistence that she would never legislate any group in the labour force back to work was sufficient to stop NDP growth. By the second debate, the angry, dismissive leader we'd seen in every other campaign and in the legislature was back. The NDP failed to close the deal with disaffected Liberal voters, including many from ethnocultural communities, who instead went to the Conservatives. The tide turned back to Ford. The NDP formed the official opposition but had missed its best opportunity in decades to win an election.

It all made no sense to me. There's not much question that my strong focus on discipline was a big reason I was no longer part of the Liberal campaign. And yet it was absence of that focus and discipline that contributed to the party's downfall. I'm well known for the saying, "Fish where the fish are." It means that in the ground game, you fight for the votes and the ridings you can get. And as hard as it is, you leave behind the ridings you just can't win.

The option would have been to determine well in advance the twenty-five to thirty ridings where we had the greatest chance. It would likely have been only long-time incumbents and in the Toronto area. It would have meant setting up elite teams and running each of the targeted ridings as we would a by-election, doing all we could to win on a riding-by-riding basis. If things were going well, we could have advanced the fight into more ridings. If they were going badly, we could pull back to the eight ridings needed to hold party status.

It would have meant giving up much earlier than Kathleen did on June 3, and accepting from the start that 2018 was lost in terms of forming a government. Instead, the goal would have been to ensure we'd have a foundation to fight in 2022, a foundation that included the extra resources that would be available in the legislature only if we had retained party status. We still would have fought as hard as we could and pushed for support. We just would have stabilized the foundation before trying to hold onto the rest of the house. And everyone involved would have known what was at stake.

There has been much speculation around the role misogyny and sexism played in the ultimate defeat of Kathleen Wynne, and in the defeat of every woman who has had a leadership role in this country since 2013. I believe many voters think a woman cannot lead a government as well as a man. I believe it's much easier and acceptable to come down hard on women, and not just politically. But to me the overarching element to consider is that in the cases when a woman was given a chance to govern, she did not meet expectations. So the real question is why the expectations have been so different for women. I don't think we really know that yet and until we find out, I fear women will continue to fall.

On the podcast "No Second Chances," Kim Campbell, the only woman to serve as prime minister of Canada (however briefly), made the following comment to host and former provincial Liberal candidate Kate Graham: "It really matters if women have power, because at the end of the day, it's governments who make decisions that bind the rest of us—and if women aren't at the table, we're not going to get what we need." It's my belief that "the table" needs more than elected officials who are women. It also needs senior advisors who are women and are in charge. Or are at least equal to men. We needed women in the room for every key decision, women charged with ensuring the real Kathleen Wynne was always at the forefront.

Although there was a woman at the top, our government was essentially run by an old boys' club. That reality was the only true barrier I encountered. A government run by Kathleen Wynne was capable of so much more. I believe she had a true desire to do things differently, but the first step would have needed to be to surround herself with people who had the same desire and priorities, and were willing to slow down long enough to get it right. It went way beyond needing to run a good government; it meant running a different government. It was an incredibly tough four years and she was the right person to lead us, but we failed to ensure she had the support around her to be the best she could be.

There was no question in my mind of the values the premier brought to government: civility, kindness, humility, responsibility, accountability. What proved elusive was applying them in a consistent way that resonated outside of the corridors of power. The failure to exhibit those values in every decision contributed to why people's sense of the premier changed during her second mandate. Had we focused on continuing to break barriers instead of sliding into the status quo, there was a chance that our inspirational leader would have had a very different reaction from the electorate.

Lesson: As a political staffer, there's only the legacy you leave behind when your day is done. Seek to be remembered as someone who made a difference.

Most political staffers spend their entire lives in the backrooms. It's designed to be that way because it's the only means by which we can truly back up the elected officials we are there to serve, and to support the cause and party we believe in. As it is the politicians who ultimately live or die by the decisions made, by necessity, political staff do our work in the name of those politicians.

It means our contributions and efforts are rarely acknowledged in the public. In the background, it may become well known when an elite staffer leads an effort or resolves an issue. But we do our work quietly and effectively, ensuring it's always an elected representative who takes the message to the public. It's what makes us a mystery to the stakeholders, the media and the general public. It makes us much more powerful than many understand, and with immense power comes significant responsibility.

Sometimes all we have is our reputations. When we get it right, we're heroes; when we fail to meet expectations, our careers are set back. We hold hands and we run the gauntlet. And in campaigns, we pull together to fight until the last ballot is counted. And because our work is behind the scenes, that's where our legacy lives, too.

When I think about my legacy, I think about the next generation of Liberals I influenced and moulded—to whom I taught the basics as I mentored them forward into more challenging roles. I think about the foundational lessons that made them ready to take over as directors, chiefs and leaders of the party. I think about being a driven person—an unapologetic workaholic and disciplinarian. I take pride in the many times I've managed to demonstrate that political chaos can be wrestled into submission, and that lost causes can be turned around into successes.

Where I've been able to ingrain those characteristics into political staff, I have been happy with the outcome, with the women and men who now shoulder the burden. And I've felt particularly proud of the young women who have gotten farther faster because of my battle to bring down the barriers. I think of the times I was unfair or mean, but I worked hard to never be mean in spirit and I apologized when I was wrong. I worked hard to be a good boss, to demonstrate there was always time to show generosity and be kind; to tell someone you understood their challenges, but to push them to always be better.

"You're Pat Sorbara," is a phrase I have heard often in my career. Recently I heard a staffer credited for having a "Pat Sorbara level of bad-ass." It's those kind of comments that have convinced me that I had an impact, that I made a difference. The Liberal Party has been the party of my life. It gave me the most amazing experiences, the utmost highs and heart-wrenching lows, the most important friendships I have. It took all of my energy and tested the limits of my skills, my courage and my determination. It has been the most rewarding and the most fun (as much as I ever did fun).

It taught me to never give up, personally or professionally, despite the odds. "Never retreat, never explain, never apologize—get the thing done and let 'em howl." The reason that Nellie McClung quote is meaningful to me? As a woman who fought to stand out in politics, who was the CEO of a successful medium-sized business and who battled my demons along the journey, that call to action made a big difference to getting through to the other side. So many times, I pushed past the naysayers, the negative energy, anything that threatened my confidence and my self-worth. I learned early on that the best option is to demonstrate what you are made of and take it from there.

Regardless of political stripe, I know what political staff are made of. And I'll always work to ensure they are recognized for their value and their commitment acknowledged. I was once asked what I would say if I could only offer only one line of advice to a new political staffer. It would be this: Step up right from the start and don't stop until you've got the job done.

Acknowledgements

The only way a politician or political staffer survives their years in politics is with the support of true believers: the people who share a commitment to the cause and who recognize the work you do on behalf of it; the friends and family to whom you turn for affirmation of who you are, who sustain you through your worst times and celebrate with you at your best; those who keep the faith, no matter what. While writing this book, my mind went often to *my* true believers, surfacing in my memory through the telling of these stories. The restrictions of space may have made it impossible to highlight more than a fraction of them, but it's my sincere hope that those not specifically named will see themselves in these pages. That said, there are some who should be mentioned by name, as without them, my career, and my life, would be much less full.

Let me first thank my editor, Silas White of Nightwood Editions. He took a chance on me and my story (as he's from BC, I was even less of a known entity to him!). I'm indebted to Silas and his team for their guidance and their commitment to this endeavour.

The book serves as a tribute to my extensive Liberal family, spread out over generations and across the country. Whether or not we connect regularly, the bond we have, forged in battle, is there. Greg Wong has always had my back and is the greatest warrior I know. I miss the sage advice of Sheila James, who taught me to defend myself. I will never forget the kindness of Bryan Stortz who stepped up at a time I had virtually no one in my corner. Mike Johnson was by my side for all of my last seven years at Queen's Park. We teamed up for every election and he was there at the end. We'd come to count the chapters of our friendship by the times we moved our boxes from office to office, to home and back again.

I met Phil Playfair through the Liberal Party. He taught me that different outlooks on life can be overcome and an enduring friendship can emerge. With wife Jacqui and sons Graeme and Iain, Phil always welcomed me and my dog Nellie with open arms. The special bond I have with Graeme (deemed by my family as "the kid I never had") gives me deep joy.

I'm grateful for the long-time support and encouragement of Vince Borg, who gave me my first my job at Queen's Park. Along with Kathy Robinson, he was an early mentor and became a close friend. Hiking through Patagonia in 2003, Kathy and I developed a bond we've never lost. She taught me the "Sherpa step"—slow, tiny steps that allowed me to regulate my breathing and keep moving forward. And when I reached the next plateau, on that mountain or in politics, she cheered me onward. She put her life on hold to take every step of the Sudbury saga with me—I'll never forget her demonstration of true friendship. David Herle was there as I earned my stripes and when I hit my career peak. He had more faith in me than I had in myself sometimes. As with David and his partner Terrie, the relationship I formed with Peter Donolo, Mary and their children has been a godsend. None of them let me doubt my integrity and all of them make me smile.

Jay Feldman taught me the discipline of choosing when to fight and when to back down. Steve Hammond taught me the value of pushing through the tough moments so, that at the end of the day, you still had laughter and each other. Leslie Kirke sacrificed a lot to be there for me through some turbulent times; she's an incredible support to many and a living testament to a reality I've long adopted, "the only way out is through."

I'm also incredibly lucky to have a family of true believers. There would be no book without Katie Dupuis, a seasoned editor and my niece. When I found myself suddenly sitting at home, she encouraged me to channel my anguish into writing down the stories I'd been telling my family for decades. Her brilliance and her immense patience over the months of this project is what got it done. Matthew Dupuis, my nephew and a talented graphic designer—he and Katie make up the two halves of Chick & Owl Design Co.—co-created the cover of this book. He holds a special place in my heart—he makes me laugh when I want to cry, and I can always count on him to track me down when I've been a bit too distant.

It all began with my parents, Lanny and Eleanor, who eventually learned to let their strong-willed middle child make her mark. My work in politics wasn't easy on them and despite the times they shook their heads at it all, I knew they were proud of me. I'm grateful to my sisters Vikki, Debby, Louise and Bernadette and my twelve nieces and nephews and their spouses, for their never-ending love and support. I have a special appreciation for my sister Vikki who has long anchored me to our family. To her and to Jake, Matt and Tracy, Katie, Rebecca and Chris, and Sarah: thank you for giving me the security of "home," manifested in Sunday dinners, kids and dogs, and dance parties (and Vikki's Sweet Marie bars!). And to my sister Bernadette who long worried about the negative aspects of politics: thanks for standing by me.

When Sudbury happened, all the true believers stepped up. The bond established through politics can quickly re-emerge in a time of need. Lyn McLeod expressed her outrage in some of the funniest notes I received. Laurel Broten reminded me of my strength. The outreach from my family and friends was overwhelming. It sustained me through every difficult moment. I was also very lucky to have lawyers Erin Dann, Bill Trudell and Brian Greenspan keeping as close a watch on my emotional well-being as they did my case. They never doubted my innocence and it was a privilege to witness their genius.

I'd be remiss in not highlighting Nellie (whose namesake Nellie McClung is a personal hero). She's been my trusty best friend through it all and her presence in my life brings me delight and comfort every day.

These are my memories and my opinions, and I take full responsibility for them. I know not everyone will remember things the same way I have. This is a collection of some of the most vivid, proudest, heartbreaking and exhilarating moments I experienced on the journey. I can only hope that future generations of staffers will find some phrase, some nugget of experience, to get them through. Because while politics is most definitely a roller coaster... what a ride. To all of my true believers, I would not be who I am without you. Thank you.

Index